T0246154

# THE JOY YOU MAKE

ALSO BY STEVEN PETROW

*Dancing Against the Darkness*

*Ending the HIV Epidemic*
(editor)

*The HIV Drug Book*
(editor)

*When Someone You Know Has AIDS*

*The Essential Book of Gay Manners and Etiquette*

*The Lost Hamptons*

*Steven Petrow's Complete Gay & Lesbian Manners*

*Stupid Things I Won't Do When I Get Old*
(with Roseann Foley Henry)

# THE JOY YOU MAKE

FIND THE SILVER LININGS—
EVEN ON YOUR DARKEST DAYS

Steven Petrow

The Open Field · Penguin Life

VIKING
An imprint of Penguin Random House LLC
penguinrandomhouse.com



The Open Field/A Penguin Life Book

THE OPEN FIELD is a registered trademark of MOS Enterprises, Inc.

Grateful acknowledgment is made for permission to reprint lines from "Joy Chose You" by Donna Ashworth from *Wild Hope*. Used with permission from Donna Ashworth.

LIBRARY OF CONGRESS CATALOGING-IN-PUBLICATION DATA

Names: Petrow, Steven, author.
Title: The joy you make / Steven Petrow.
Description: New York : The Open Field, [2024]
Identifiers: LCCN 2024012263 (print) | LCCN 2024012264 (ebook) |
ISBN 9780593654224 (hardcover) | ISBN 9780593654231 (ebook)
Subjects: LCSH: Joy.
Classification: LCC BF575.H27 P4548 2024 (print) | LCC BF575.H27 (ebook) |
DDC 152.4/2—dc23/eng/20240603
LC record available at https://lccn.loc.gov/2024012263
LC ebook record available at https://lccn.loc.gov/2024012264

Printed in the United States of America
1st Printing

DESIGNED BY MEIGHAN CAVANAUGH

MARIA SHRIVER

PRESENTS

# THE OPEN FIELD

A PUBLISHING IMPRINT

BOOKS THAT RISE ABOVE THE NOISE AND MOVE HUMANITY FORWARD

Dear Reader,

Years ago, these words attributed to Rumi found a place in my heart:

*Out beyond ideas of*
*wrongdoing and rightdoing,*
*there is a field. I'll meet you there.*

Ever since, I've cultivated an image of what I call "the Open Field"—a place out beyond fear and shame, beyond judgment, loneliness, and expectation. A place that hosts the reunion of all creation. It's the hope of my soul to find my way there—and whenever I hear an insight or a practice that helps me on the path, I love nothing more than to share it with others.

That's why I've created The Open Field. My hope is to publish books that honor the most unifying truth in human life: We are all seeking the same things. We're all seeking dignity. We're all seeking joy. We're all seeking love and acceptance, seeking to be seen, to be safe. And there is no competition for these things we seek—because they are not material goods; they are spiritual gifts!

We can all give each other these gifts if we share what we know—what has lifted us up and moved us forward. That is our duty to one another—to help each other toward acceptance, toward peace, toward happiness—and my promise to you is that the books published under this imprint will be maps to the Open Field, written by guides who know the path and want to share it.

Each title will offer insights, inspiration, and guidance for moving beyond the fears, the judgments, and the masks we all wear. And when we take off the masks, guess what? We will see that we are the opposite of what we thought—we are each other.

We are all on our way to the Open Field. We are all helping one another along the path. I'll meet you there.

Love, Maria S

*For my beautiful sister, Julie,*

*who lived a full life by any measure,*

*and who shared her joy with everyone she met*

[J]oy is *supposed* to slither through
the cracks of your imperfect life
that's how joy *works*

[Y]ou cannot truly invite her
you can only be ready
when she appears
and hug her with meaning
because in this very moment
joy chose you.

Donna Ashworth,
"Joy Chose You" in *Wild Hope*

They find a remedy because
they seek it together.

Émile Durkheim

# CONTENTS

# AUTHOR'S NOTE

Some of the stories and reporting in these pages appeared previously in columns I wrote for *The Washington Post* and *The New York Times*. To protect certain individuals' privacy, a few names have been changed or omitted.

# INTRODUCTION

A little consideration, a little thought for others, makes all the difference.

EEYORE

My mother died on a snowy evening in 2017, right after New Year's. My dad passed away three months later. In between those two losses, my husband moved out of our house. Before the year had ended, my sister, Julie, had been diagnosed with stage four ovarian cancer. So I'm not overstating things to say that 2017 was a truly grievous year for my family and me.

Long before the events of 2017, I'll admit I was already a glass-half-empty kind of guy, with a dark cloud hovering over me. (Some of my friends even call me Eeyore, the gloomy jackass in the Winnie-the-Pooh books.) I've also been called out as a curmudgeon, which is to say a midlife crank (long before I turned fifty) or a sourpuss. On top of that, I often felt as though my life was on autopilot. I was not fully engaged, unhappy for no particular reason. When I first read Angela Williams Gorrell's book *The Gravity of Joy*, I felt a sense of connection and kinship, particularly at the part where she writes, "Many of us don't sense joy. We don't know how to become open to it, how to seek it, or how to share our longing for it. And often, even when it comes, we do not feel free to express it."

Yet, with all this baggage, in the midst of the darkness of 2017, I surprised myself when I began to experience the tiniest sparks of joy. (Imagine that: me, Eeyore!) One afternoon, I spontaneously snapped a photo of a brilliant sunset, posting it on Instagram with the hashtags #gratitude and #beautyiseverywhere. Soon enough, I'd begun a regular practice of taking and posting photographs—of beauties like sun- and moonrises, flowers and fields, but even of a brick wall overlooking a parking area with humorous graffiti that read "Bark here." Each time, I enjoyed what I've now come to think of as a "joy hit."

At first I thought my practice was just about taking pretty or amusing pictures. Then I believed it was about seeking and noting beauty in the everyday. Eventually, as more and more friends responded and began posting their own photos with the hashtag #gratitude, I understood that a big chunk of my joy came from sharing with others. I continued this practice throughout the pandemic, right up until now. The pictures never fail to delight me—to connect me with my friends, and them with me. Even though I didn't realize it at the time, I had started my search for joy.

In my work as a journalist, essayist, and book author, I've long tried to extrapolate deeper life lessons from everyday experiences. With the pandemic winter of 2022 hitting us all hard, I decided to take a stab at better understanding joy, writing a column for *The Washington Post* titled simply enough, "How I found joy in life during difficult times." The piece touched a nerve, quickly becoming one of the week's most-read stories. And why not? By that time we'd been locked in at home, shut out of the workplace, isolated and disconnected from friends and family for almost two years. More than a million Americans had died from Covid-19. If that weren't enough, the divides within families and communities had only deepened due to polarized opinions over mask and vaccine efficacy, climate change, and the 2020 election results. We had a mess on our hands.

Oh, and my sister fell out of remission that winter, leading to a new surge of uncertainty.

In the *Post* I wrote that "the past twenty-two months haven't registered high on what I'd call the joy-o-meter," which was an understatement for sure.

Poll after poll confirmed what many had experienced. One of them, a Kaiser Family Foundation study, reported that four in ten U.S. adults had experienced symptoms of anxiety or depression during the coronavirus pandemic, up from one in ten in 2019, with the most vulnerable among us—racial minorities, sexual minorities, the poor, older people, and younger people—at greatest risk.

Despite the overwhelming sadness and suffering many were experiencing, I also read a surprising poll published by the University of Michigan called "Joy and Stress during the COVID-19 Pandemic." It reported that 83 percent of adults over fifty had felt "some" or "a lot" of joy since March 2020, the official beginning of the pandemic. That statistic knocked me in the head, as it also did one of the lead researchers, Jessica Finlay, a faculty fellow at the Institute of Behavioral Science at the University of Colorado Boulder. She acknowledged her surprise at the findings, explaining to me, "It's not a monolithic story of decline or loss. People are finding silver linings in this time and are resilient to what they're experiencing."

And there it was. Joy is always present—in the silver lining, in the resiliency, in our memories, in the connection to those who share your grief when it comes. It's in the everyday world, on good days as well as bad ones. You only have to look for it, be confident that it's there, and be open to it when you find it.

I asked Finlay for some examples of joy in her life. She did not miss a beat: spending time outside, hearing birdsong in the morning, and most of all receiving a big hug from a family member after months of isolation. Listening to her, I began to see how these small joys sustained her, reminding me of my own practice of taking and posting photographs—also small joys that had buoyed me through my hardest year and beyond. I conducted an informal survey among Facebook friends, asking them, "How have you found joy in these difficult times?" The answers lifted me and, frankly, made me smile. Among the hundreds of responses, these caught my attention: adopting a hamster "who lives in a hamster mansion," spending time with the grandchildren, streaming British comedies, eating chocolates, making a daily gratitude list, dancing, writing poetry, baking cookies, volunteering, cycling, enjoying the solitude, and—my favorite—reveling in "the unpredictability of autocorrect." The deeper themes weren't hard to see: connection, humor, helping others, gratitude, kindness, movement, and consuming lots of calories.

A month or so after my *Post* essay on joy had appeared, my literary agent called. "There's a publisher who would like to know if you can write a book about joy for her. She read your *Post* column. What do you think?" I wrestled with the question for a few days, asking myself whether I had the right mindset to write a book about finding and cultivating joy in challenging times. I'd read other works about joy written by poets and prophets, mystics and magicians. More recently, scholars and academics have focused their pointy heads on joy, adding to our understanding but often squeezing the life—the joy—right out of it. What I hadn't read was anything practical about how to navigate difficult days (and years). A book that simultaneously acknowledges the truly dreadful events we all go through, often under lingering clouds of sadness and despair, and points us to those little nuggets of joy.

I started to think: Maybe I *am* the right person to research and write a book about joy. After all, I'm a pretty regular guy (gay) who drinks bourbon (straight up), loves games (especially winning), and keeps busy (too much for my own good). But I'm also curious, generally kind, with a pretty good sense of humor (especially about myself). I love my family, and I have a wonderful set of friends. But something has always been missing. For most of my adult life I've struggled to feel more joyful—to *be* more joyful—sometimes chasing it, sometimes despairing of ever finding it, other times too lost to see it right in front of me. So maybe, just maybe, I could bring a fresh perspective to the search for joy—especially when it seems so elusive.

I decided I could write this book because this was a search I needed to undertake for myself. To boot, if eight in ten Americans over fifty had been on the joy train in the previous two years, I wanted to find out how they did that, join them, and then tell others.

That's how this book came to be—its origin story, if you will. I hope you'll accompany me on this excursion. I will say this now, before you get started: You don't need to go to an expensive retreat center or an eco-friendly, carbon-neutral destination to find joy. You don't have to get a new job, buy a new car, or take a faraway vacation. You don't even need to sit, legs crossed and eyes closed, breathing in and out, counting to ten, one hundred—or what sometimes feels like one thousand—and then back to zero. You don't need to do any of that, because that's not where joy resides.

So what *can* you do to experience more joy?

I went to work, digesting a steady diet of books, articles, podcasts, and videos. I interviewed dozens of experts—psychologists, social scientists, religious leaders, ethicists, and others—who shared with me their perspectives on how we can find joy in our lives, cultivate it, share it, and be open to receiving it.

And I turned to writers like Andrew Holleran (author of *Grief*), Nikki Erlick (author of *The Measure*), and Elizabeth Gilbert (author of *Eat Pray Love*), who can hardly put pen to paper without touching on some shade of joy (and its first cousins: sorrow, loss, and grief). I read many poems by Mary Oliver (author of *Winter Hours*, *Dog Songs*, and *Dream Work*) and Christian Wiman's amazing anthology of poems, *Joy*, that includes everyone from Gertrude Stein and Gwendolyn Brooks to Paul Celan and Yehuda Amichai.

I learned a lot, starting with: Joy is not only around us, but within us. It inhabits the present, the past, and even the future as we look toward it. We often don't recognize joy because it's no one-note wonder, which is to say that so many different types of joy exist—serene, ecstatic, sexual, even schadenfreude (the pleasure derived from another person's misfortune). It goes by many names, including delight, exuberance, pleasure, peace, contentedness, amusement, wonder, relief, bliss, pride, and gratitude. It can even be found within grief and sorrow.

For sure, my joy may not be constant (it ebbs and flows over a lifetime), just as it may not be yours. But here's what makes me so excited about joy: It doesn't require any special skills or talents. It's widely available—anyone or, more to the point, everyone can experience joy. But, yes, it does take practice. Yes, it does mean shifting our perspective about how we want to live. Yes, it means saying to yourself, "I choose joy."

One of my favorite novelists, Barbara Kingsolver, writes about the challenge of finding joy in her novel *High Tide in Tucson*. This passage has long been the nexus of my search:

> In my own worst seasons I've come back from the colorless world of despair by forcing myself to look hard, for a long time, at a single glorious thing: a flame of red geranium outside my bedroom window. And then another: my daughter in a yellow dress. And another: the perfect outline of a full, dark sphere behind the crescent moon. Until I learned to be in love with my life again. Like a stroke victim retraining new parts of the brain to grasp lost skills, I have taught myself joy, over and over again.

Is all of this easy? I'll be honest—sometimes it is, but not every day. In the many years I've been on this path, I can truthfully say I am living with more joy than ever before, even after the deaths of my parents, my separation and divorce, and my sister's illness. As Angela Williams Gorrell writes, "Grief doesn't just vanish because joy comes. Instead, joy has a mysterious capacity to be felt alongside sorrow and even—sometimes most especially—in the midst of suffering." Put another way, joy is the great unifier.

This book is the personal story of the search I undertook, and what I learned, which I hope will help you see more clearly where joy lives within you and around you, in the darkness and the light, in the present and the future.

Please join me.

# What Do We Mean When We Talk About Joy?

Before I can ask you to read a book about joy, we need to agree on what it is. In this sense I was lucky to have grown up with a father who was a journalist and professor. He was my first (and to this day toughest) editor. He would often prod me to define my terms, and I can hear him now, using my childhood nickname: "Steverino, you're writing a book about joy. What is joy?"

Let me start with what it is not: happiness.

I often joke that there's a "happiness-industrial complex" in twenty-first-century America. We're drowning in happiness—with books like *The Happiness Advantage; The Happiness Trap; You, Happier; The Art of Happiness; How Happiness Happens;* and even the Peanuts book series *Happiness Is. . . .* Happiness has been dissected and unpacked, analyzed and quantified—and, no surprise, monetized. That's a lot of happiness.

Joy has gotten so much less attention than its shinier and brighter first cousin. Adam Potkay, a professor at the College of William & Mary and the author of many books, including *The Story of Joy*, observes that "joy is a word we don't use much anymore, at least not in secular contexts." In the last century, he points out, "the word did not fare well in poetry, politics, or ordinary conversation." As a telling example he cites the playwright George Bernard Shaw, who used "happy" seven times more than "joy."

But joy, I believe, is more sustaining and gratifying than happiness. One way I like to describe this difference is to think of happiness as a sugary Twinkie, with joy more like a whole wheat muffin. The Twinkie boosts your glucose levels, resulting in a sugar high, and then you crash. The healthier muffin is metabolized more slowly, with no big high or low, leaving you satisfied for a longer time.

I'm not alone in making this distinction. Archbishop Desmond Tutu wrote pointedly in *The Book of Joy,* "Joy is much bigger than happiness. While happiness is often seen as being dependent on external circumstances, joy is not." In the same book, His Holiness the Dalai Lama responds to his co-author, "Yes, it is true. Joy is something different from happiness." He goes on to explain that even a painful experience, say childbirth, "can bring great satisfaction and joyfulness." This is to say that joy is, as one reviewer of the book noted, "a conscious choice to respond to our circumstances in a positive and fulfilling way. We cannot change our circumstances, but we can change how we respond."

Adela Rogers St. Johns, one of the best-known reporters of the early twentieth century who frequently wrote about the underbelly of urban life, described how she understood the difference between happiness and joy: "Joy seems to me a step beyond happiness—happiness is a sort of atmosphere you can live in sometimes when you're lucky. Joy is a light that fills you with hope and faith and love."

But it's Robert Emmons whom I turned to repeatedly

during my search. Emmons is perhaps the preeminent expert on joy these days—he's the author of five books, including *The Psychology of Gratitude,* and founder and editor in chief of *The Journal of Positive Psychology*. He, too, writes about how these two states differ. "Happiness is an inch deep and a mile wide, whereas joy is a mile deep and a mile wide."

Okay, now that we've defined what joy *isn't*—it's *not* happiness—what *is* joy?

Dating all the way back to the eleventh century, the word itself is derived from the Old French *joie* ("pleasure, delight, erotic pleasure, bliss, joyfulness") and the Latin *gaudia* ("expressions of pleasure; sensual delight"), as well as from *gaudere* ("rejoice"). *The Oxford English Dictionary* calls it, without much ado (or joy), "a feeling of great pleasure and happiness." (One critic commented that this definition was like describing champagne as "a bubbly liquid, but forgetting all about its golden colour, whiffs of ripe pear and fresh baked bread in its aroma or traces of apple, vanilla, yeast and nuts in its flavour, and, of course, its capacity to intoxicate.")

Just about everyone seems to have their own idea of what joy is. Adam Potkay likely knows more about the history and etymology of joy than almost anyone else, dead or alive. In *The Story of Joy*, Potkay carefully outlines its many forms, including spiritual joy, religious joy, erotic joy, vulgar joy, ethereal joy, fearful joy, evil joy, and anxious joy, among others, suggesting quite clearly that our one-dimensional view of joy is a blurred perspective.

I, like many, long thought of joy as a single note. Call it ecstasy, a kind of big bang—what you feel watching the bombs bursting in air on July Fourth, experiencing the first flush and rush of a new love, and singing out loud and off-key any song by Cher (but especially "Believe"). After my niece Jessie was asked to officiate at the wedding of her two best friends, she wrote in an essay: "How to express the joy this incites in me. Words like 'implode,' 'explode,' 'burst,' 'erupt.' The sensation of the uncontainable. Joy that is physically seeping out of my seams and through my eyes, which, yes, I've confirmed, are crying. . . ." All-powerful joy. Overwhelming joy. Joy that takes up every inch of space in our bodies.

But, as I've learned on my journey, this kind of ecstatic joy is but one kind or flavor—one that overshadows, even eclipses, the many other types of joy.

One of the most comprehensive studies of the different forms of joy took place in the 1970s when Chris M. Meadows, a clinical psychologist and psychotherapist who taught at Vanderbilt University, sorted through thousands of accounts of joyful experiences from more than three hundred college students. Meadows eventually established that there are three dimensions of joyful experience, which has greatly helped me to understand this multifaceted emotion. First, there's what Meadows describes as "excited" joy (intense and high energy, or "powerful") versus "serene" joy (mellow and calm, giving feelings of harmony and unity, or "quiet delight"). Meadows also looked at what he calls "individuated" versus "affiliative" joy, by which he means joy experienced solo as opposed to joy that is shared with others. (More than 70 percent of the joyful experiences reported in his study took place in social settings.) Finally, there's what he refers to as "anticipatory" joy, when the fulfillment of some desire appears to be imminent, versus "consummatory" joy, when the desire has been fulfilled.

If anything, "joys are plural and variegated," as Potkay emphasizes repeatedly, and which Meadows's research clearly supports.

Despite my dad's admonition to define my terms, I often believe examples are more helpful, especially when it comes to making distinctions. Because joy is so varied and can feel elusive, these comparisons may help us to better understand how it manifests, boosting our awareness, which in turn allows us to better experience it. Here are some of the ways I've come to see joy, compared with happiness:

**Happiness** is eating a fudge brownie.

**Joy** is making a pan of brownies to share.

**Happiness** is a highly charged kiss.

**Joy** is the sense of connection or oneness that comes from trust and intimacy.

**Happiness** is buying the red sports car you've always wanted.

**Joy** is the experience you gain when traveling. (And if you do so in your new sports car, there's no reason you can't hold both happiness and joy together.)

**Happiness** is learning that you've gone into remission, or—even better—been cured of a scary disease.

**Joy** is holding the hand of a loved one going through such an illness, even if they don't get well. (That's why joy and sorrow can cohabit in our hearts; happiness does not play well with other emotions.)

And one last example for now:

**Happiness** is about me.

**Joy** is about we, which is to say, you and me.

It took me a while to come to my own definition of joy, but now I see it. Gratitude. Connection. Generosity. Kindness. Empathy. These are the necessary ingredients. The joys we experience come from the combination of these five states or traits. Tinker with the recipe and you change what form the joy takes—ecstatic joy, quiet-delight joy, et cetera—though it will always be joy.

Now that we're beginning to understand the multitude of ways that joy can manifest, how do we find it? How do we embrace it? How can we cultivate it? Share it? That's what I wanted to know when I set out to write this book, and the pages that follow chronicle all that I've learned along the way.

# THE JOY OF GRATITUDE

I've referred to 2017 as my "annus horribilis," and justifiably so. Queen Elizabeth II made that expression famous in 1992, when the royals suffered multiple marital dramas and a castle fire to boot. Twenty-five years later the Windsors had nothing on me. In the midst of my turmoil, I started taking and then posting photographs on Instagram that I tagged #gratitude and #beautyiseverywhere; I found myself genuinely, surprisingly grateful to have experienced their beauty.

Sometimes beauty took other, less conventional forms. One afternoon the darkest cloud I can remember descended from the heavens, bringing with it torrential rains and a majestic display of thunder and lightning. I pulled out my phone and snapped the falling sky. How could I not feel gratitude for witnessing such an awesome show of nature? How could I not recall this sentence from Edith Wharton: "There are two ways of spreading light; to be the candle or the mirror that reflects it"?

Several months later, on a walk in my neighborhood, I passed by a dilapidated local church desperately in need of a paint job, yet decked out in its Christmas finery. I experienced gratitude in witnessing the resilience of both the church building and its supportive members.

As friends and followers responded, thanking me not only for sharing these photos but also for this way of seeing light in the darkness, grit amidst the ruins, my gratitude deepened. Even more surprising, I felt spasms of joy emanating from this gratefulness.

I came to understand what researchers have been focused on in recent years: gratitude is foundational to the experience of joy. Madeline R. Greaves's thesis, "A Prospective Investigation of Joy and Trait Gratitude," explains further: "One may not be able to 'choose' to experience joy," she writes. "However . . . one may prepare for joy, or prime oneself through thoughts and behaviors to allow joy to more likely be experienced. One such way of preparing for joy might be in having a grateful mindset." In other words, simply being open to gratitude likely helps us to feel joy.

Greaves explains that "trait gratitude" refers to a person's predisposition to feel grateful. As other researchers have noted, some people simply have an innate predisposition for gratitude or a grateful outlook. You know the type of people I'm talking about: they seek the good around them; they see "all of life as a gift" or they count their blessings. Others seem constitutionally less disposed to gratitude: we have a more cynical bent and don't always see "silver linings." But if I understand Greaves correctly, anyone—even those of us who aren't predisposed to it—can learn to feel more grateful, which paves a path to joy.

At the same time, many scholars believe joy is important for cultivating gratitude. If you can't see the good in the world coming from sources outside of yourself, you're going to find yourself low on any measure of gratefulness. Together, joy and gratitude have a reciprocal, or symbiotic, relationship that can "result in an upward spiral that enhances well-being," writes Philip Watkins, a professor of psychology at Eastern Washington University and a researcher in an important 2020 study of gratitude and joy.

Truth be told, ever since 2017 it had been hard for me to feel grateful for what I have. I was focusing more on my current sorrows and prospective losses. Still, I wanted to experience more gratitude, especially since it's known as the "social glue" that strengthens relationships of all kinds, even serving "as the backbone of human society," according to the Greater Good Science Center at the University of California, Berkeley. And while a significant part of me is Eeyore, I'm also a little bit Tigger, another Pooh character, known for his black-on-orange stripes, large eyes, springy tail, and a love of bouncing. Tigger is cheerful, outgoing, competitive in a friendly way, and has complete confidence in himself. (As I said, I'm only a little bit Tigger.) How could I become more like Tigger? How could I cultivate my gratitude?

I first learned about Robert Emmons, dubbed "the world's leading scientific expert on gratitude," more than a decade ago when I read an article of his titled "Why Gratitude Is Good," wherein he writes about helping "people systematically cultivate gratitude."

His perspective hasn't changed since then, as he explained in a more recent public lecture. "One of the best practices for developing joy or finding joy is practicing gratitude," he told Matt Croasmun in a talk called "Theology of Joy" at a Yale Divinity School conference. He added, "When a person cultivates a sense of appreciation, a sense of wonder, a sense of aliveness and vitality, it seems to be a very reliable way of developing more joy."

Toward the end of his conversation, Emmons quoted the British writer G. K. Chesterton, who apparently had given much thought to gratitude, concluding, "Gratitude is happiness doubled by wonder." Emmons took the equation a step further, noting that "joy is happiness doubled by gratitude." He continued, "Gratitude gives us that connection. It gives us that sense of transcendence, the sense of celebration, but also the awareness of the finiteness of life." Other scholars have made much the same point about joy: joy is rooted in connection.

Fortunately, Emmons's approach to cultivating gratitude is simple. He recommends keeping a gratitude journal, a simple notebook, to regularly record the things for which we're grateful. Would I have very much—or anything—to record? I wouldn't know unless I tried.

Sometimes serendipity swoops in like an owl sighting a mouse. Soon after my mom died, I was browsing at one of my favorite local bookstores and picked up a very slim paperback called

*The Mindfulness Journal*, created by David de Souza, a meditation teacher. Each day and every page is the same, with several prompts to be completed by bedtime. How do you feel? What exercise did you do? Did you meditate? And, at the bottom of the page: What are you grateful for today?

For five dollars I bought one of the booklets, which stressed the importance of intention and consistency in this practice of cultivating gratitude. Despite my concern that I'd have nothing to be grateful for, I surprised myself. In that first brown booklet (yes, I wound up buying many) I answered the last question with entries such as "laughter," "Julie and Maddy" (my sister and sister-in-law), "granola and sushi" (not together), "the moon," "swimming," "the smell of the rain," and a number of friends I'd spent time with.

It was not so hard after all, although my gratitude was also not exactly earth-shattering; actually, it seemed destined to remain the lowercase variety. When I talked with de Souza, I mentioned the ordinariness of my gratefulness. He replied, "It doesn't need to be [extraordinary]. In fact, the smaller the better, as it helps to uncover things that you may never have noticed, giving you the opportunity to show appreciation and be happy." I continued on with entries like "a beautiful thunderstorm," "intimacy" (with someone I won't name here!), "the quiet," "feeling the sun," and so on.

Okay, but I worried: Would this work in another annus horribilis, as our first pandemic year was shaping up to be? When I spoke with de Souza in 2021, he readily admitted that if "we zoom out and look back over 2020 we might think there's little to be grateful for." If that year had been a song, he said, it would have been "a sad melody." He suggested, instead, that "we zoom in and focus on the individual notes that make up the song." Even in the darkest days, he argued, we'll find "small gestures or notes that are worthy sources of gratitude." I'm now remembering the countless acts of goodness and kindness, like New York City's nightly seven p.m. cheer for frontline workers, and Toronto's "caremongering," when strangers gave food away to those in need, or offered to foster pets and pick up medications.

Recent studies support the idea that grateful people are able to experience joy even in the most challenging of situations. One research subject told an interviewer, "Even when things aren't going well, I can still feel joy." Similarly, Stacy Batten explained to *The New York Times* how, in 2022, her husband died from cancer, her father died from Parkinson's disease, and her mother learned she had cancer—but Batten realized that in seeking the good parts of each day, she felt better. She did this by writing on scraps of paper and dropping them in a mason jar she called her "gratitude jar." She noted, "The grief is still there but writing those daily notes has helped."

As it turns out, de Souza was right. Now half a dozen years and many, many five-dollar brown booklets later, I've found at least one thing to be grateful for each day—often two or three. Emmons has written that gratitude journals and other gratitude practices "often seem so simple and basic," but they work. In a white paper titled *The Science of Gratitude*, Emmons and other researchers reported that even if we only keep gratitude journals for three weeks, the effects of gratitude on physical health, psychological well-being, and personal relationships are overwhelming—

from lower blood pressure and stronger immune systems to less fatigue and greater resilience. Gratitude, it seems, makes one more helpful and compassionate while feeling less lonely and isolated.

I now fall asleep most nights conscious of the good that enveloped me each day, or that just barely touched me, and how it made a difference to my well-being. I feel more patient, sleep better, and overall seem happier—all benefits that studies suggest gratitude can engender. Sometimes, once in bed, I'll listen to meditation teacher Jeff Warren's short meditation called "Nightly Gratitude" on the Ten Percent Happier app. He begins by admitting that the whole idea sounded cheesy to him at the outset, but no more. Why's that? Because it helped him. He extols listeners—no matter how awesome or crappy our days may be—to think back to one thing that was good. I especially appreciated that Jeff emphasizes "It doesn't matter how small the thing is."

On the day my father died I couldn't imagine what I had to be grateful for. My father had been a man full of secrets and anger, a husband and father who did not know how to connect with his family. If I'd been asked to describe my relationship with Dad, I'd have said (kindly), "It's complicated." Still, late that evening, exhausted, I opened my brown notebook and began to scribble. The first two items came easily enough: "The support of my brother and sister during Dad's illness," followed by, "The peace I hope Dad has now found." Then I had to stretch a bit, which was okay, writing, "The chocolate ice cream that neighbors brought over."

By the time I turned out the light, I felt more at peace with Dad's death (although not with his life). Some researchers, like Philip Watkins, suggest "joy is the result of the perception that life is going well and life is being lived well." That night I could say that my life had turned out well. For that I felt grateful, and—odd as it may sound—I also experienced equanimity, or a subdued contentedness, another way to describe joy.

## How to Cultivate More Gratitude

I have learned from personal experience that gratitude is a building block for joy—but it doesn't always come naturally. My nightly gratitude journal entries felt a little forced in the beginning, but they blossomed into a joyous record of all that's good in life. Those joys exist even on the darkest of days, and remembering to be grateful for them is a habit you can develop.

**Step one** is awareness of those good things. That may sound self-evident, but it can be so easy to drown in negative thoughts that it may take a conscious effort to focus on the positive. Pick a time every day to stop and reflect on at least one thing you have to be grateful for that day. What did you see, hear, smell, taste, or feel that is a reason for gratitude? If you're having trouble conjuring something, Robert Emmons suggests thinking back on a bad experience as a way to see how far you've come, or looking at photos of people and places you love and for which you are grateful.

**Step two** is recording these moments somewhere. I used my nightly journal and my Instagram posts. Cathy Hankla, a professor emerita of English and creative writing at Hollins University and a well-known poet, got through the early pandemic isolation by posting daily

"Miracle Reports"—photos of nature, food she'd prepared, or everyday events that made her feel joy—which she said could easily have been called daily "Gratitude Reports." Think of ways you can record your daily joys: by writing them down, taking photos, making voice recordings, or even posting to social media. It doesn't matter how you record them; the important thing is keeping a record so you can see how every day provides a reason to feel grateful.

**Step three** is sharing your gratitude. Say thank you to someone who holds a door for you. Call a friend you've been out of touch with. If you took a photo of something that brought you joy, consider sending that photo to a loved one along with a brief message. Maybe you'll end up in that person's gratitude journal tonight!

# THE JOY OF AUTHENTICITY

I have a black-and-white photograph of myself on the mantel in my office; it's an outtake from a professional shoot my parents organized of my brother, my sister, and me when I was about ten. For many years I had it taped to the bathroom mirror so that I'd see it first thing every morning. It's long been a reminder to myself of happy times.

In the photo I'm sticking my tongue out—playfully. My eyes are full of light. The two cowlicks on my head wreak havoc with my hair (as they will for my whole life, no matter how much product I use to tamp them down), but they are central to me, resilient and whimsical.

I know this boy is me—but I do not recognize him. There's an easiness, spontaneity, and yes, authenticity defining him.

To all appearances, I'd been an average American preteen, like one of the *Brady Bunch* boys. As I grew older, I learned to camouflage my real self, my essence.

Our family spent summers at a beach colony on Long Island. By the time I turned fourteen, I'd begun to hide my real self from others, and from myself. That year, which would have been 1971, I dressed in the thick white belt and bell-bottoms my mom had bought in London, and I walked over to the home of a neighbor—a woman who'd never married and was in her eighties. I introduced myself as Iggy, a transplanted orphan from London, whose parents ("They were both m-m-musicians," I stammered on purpose) and siblings ("I m-m-miss them so m-m-much") had died in a horrid car accident. On each visit, this kind lady would serve Earl Grey tea and shortbread, and I'd listen attentively to the lonely truth of her days—present and past—and fabricate mine.

I knew enough about my namesake, rocker Iggy Pop, to spin a tale darkly. A famous singer who had traveled the world, the "Godfather of Punk" had been a drug addict known for self-mutilation who, as part of his onstage act, often exposed himself and vomited, threw himself into the audience, and then rolled around on glass shards. One afternoon, in character as Iggy, I told her my father had sexually abused me before his tragic demise. This was all, of course, not true. But looking back from the present, I realize I found a way of telling my truth by, well, not telling the truth. I had a dark secret that I'd yet to reveal, so out of the desire to be seen and heard, I concocted a way of revealing my truth.

Finally, at summer's end, my mother—alive and well—bumped into our neighbor, who told her about this lovely young man, recounting my very *Annie* tale of misfortune. "Where does he live?" Mom asked. The neighbor pointed to our house. Once home, Mom squeezed every last detail out of me, and then sent me back over to confess my wrenching set of lies, and I never saw my elderly friend again. For years I continued to think of *her* as the mother who protected me, who understood me, who listened to me. A mother who could accept a gangly, messed-up fourteen-year-old, which was exactly how I saw myself.

One cold spring morning about ten years ago, I found that someone had slipped a book into my mail slot at the Virginia Center for the Creative Arts, where I was a writer in residence. It was a copy of Carrie Brown's novel *The Last First Day.* The text on the dust jacket got my attention: "Here is the story of a woman's life in its twilight, as she looks back on a harrowing childhood and on the unaccountable love and happiness that emerged from it." I jumped into the book, putting my own writing aside for the morning in my eagerness to learn how Ruth, the protagonist, overcame the challenges of her youth.

To this day I'm not sure if the novel was meant for someone else or if I had been the designated recipient, with the gift giver preferring to stay anonymous. No matter how or why, I am thankful, because that 304-page book became my primer in seeking to live a more authentic life.

Toward the end of Brown's page-turner, I came to this line: "If I can't ever tell anyone the true story . . . then no one will ever know me." I hung on to those words. I also thought back to that black-and-white photo of a young me, with those happy eyes, an easeful smile, and a nose that looked as though it could twitch. That boy in the photo is full of life and joy; this man in midlife was not.

I find myself writing about that boy instinctively in the third person, as though he's not really me. In later photos, my smile seems unnatural, almost forced. The twinkle in my eyes is dimmed. It's as though my true nature has been hidden—or worse, erased. For a long time I wondered what happened to him.

At the time I read Carrie Brown's novel, I happened to be working on an essay about my coming out as a gay man. But I was having a difficult time writing it, snagged in that very same way as when I had come to Ruth's prophesy. Would I tell my *true* story?

I don't believe in coincidences, although I do in serendipity. I thought there must have been a reason why I couldn't let go of Brown's prescient sentence just as I was trying to write my story for the very first time. I'd been a raconteur and a chameleon my entire life, which left me with a short stick when it came to authenticity—the quality that Jean-Paul Sartre pointedly once wrote is fundamental to living a meaningful life.

Brian Goldman and Michael Kernis, two psychologists, define authenticity as "the unimpeded operation of one's true- or core-self in one's daily enterprise." *The Stanford Encyclopedia of Philosophy* goes further: "[T]he characterization [of someone as authentic] describes a person who acts in accordance with desires, motives, ideals or beliefs that are not only hers (as opposed to someone else's), but that also express who she really is." I have to admit, I especially like how the Society of American Archivists defines the word in relation to documents but with relevance to humans: "The quality of being genuine, not a counterfeit, and free from tampering, and is typically inferred from internal and external evidence, including its physical characteristics, structure, content, and context."

Living an inauthentic life has its costs, among them isolation, lack of connection, and not knowing your real self. In living a truthful life, a genuine one or an authentic one, we're allowed to remove our masks of pretense, fakery, and people-pleasing, the doing of which can boost self-esteem and bring a sense of real peace, contentment, connection, serenity, and yes, joy. In his book *Be Yourself, Everyone Else Is Already Taken,* Mike Robbins explains that being open and transparent—honest—allows for deeper connections with others, which, in turn, engages others to be more comfortable and vulnerable in revealing their true selves.

A year after receiving Carrie Brown's book, I finally wrote this sentence into my coming out essay: "I had been molested as a child."

Getting to the point where I could even consider putting those seven words down on paper had taken a lifetime.

I'd made some earlier attempts. In 1989, when I was thirty-two years old, I confided my secret to one of my closest friends, who in turn revealed to me her own experiences of being sexually abused. Tragically, within the year, my friend—only twenty-six—died by suicide. I was alone with my secret yet again.

Soon after, I made another attempt at disclosure, confiding in a new boyfriend who seemed to love and accept me despite the stained soul that I saw in the mirror. But he betrayed me, and when I moved out, he sent a postcard (a postcard!) to my office announcing a meeting of sexual abuse survivors at my apartment. The so-called invitation, he threatened, would also be mailed to my entire family unless I agreed to move back in with him.

Soon after that breakup, I made an appointment with a psychotherapist. For several visits I dutifully went to his office but couldn't answer the question "Why are you here?" Finally, this is what I wrote down and then read out loud to him:

> As much as I have tried, I can't actually say to you what I need to without reading the words from this paper. . . . I'm afraid to read this because in telling you the story it will become real. But, I need to become real. I'm ready.

I read to him the details of what my paternal grandfather did to me as a young boy, ending with:

> I don't know where all of that fear went. It just stayed inside me. I buried it that quickly and that perfectly.

I continued in therapy and made quiet disclosures to a few of my closest friends. I continued to have dreams, frightening ones.

Over two decades, I talked to those whom I trusted about revealing more—but why? My grandfather was dead. I was married. "I don't need anything from anyone" became my constant refrain.

Until the day when I realized I did need something. I'd previously come out as gay and then later as a cancer survivor, two identities that carry some measure of stigma and shame. I'd seen how shedding a skin had always made a positive difference in how I felt about myself—and in deepening my relationships.

My friend and confidante Amy wrote me: "You're tired of holding your secret, you want it to come out and you'll deal with whatever fallout there may be. It's time."

Before the publication of my coming out essay, I told my sister, then my brother, both of whom instinctively supported me. Finally, I went to see my parents, then in their eighties and not in the best of health. I'd thought about this conversation a hundred times before, but this was no dress rehearsal. When I finished, my mom, a retired psychiatric social worker, put on her professional hat and said: "Sexual abuse is all too common and hidden away."

The healing power of my family's love and support was immediately tangible. I'd finally allowed myself to be vulnerable. In *Daring Greatly*, Brené Brown writes, "Vulnerability is the birthplace of love, belonging, joy, courage, empathy, and creativity. It is the source of hope, empathy, accountability, and authenticity."

A few weeks later my true story, which included those revelatory seven words, was published.

Since then I've received numerous messages praising my honesty, my authenticity. My good friend Peter sent an email, reading in part:

> Life seems to be a continual act of coming out, isn't it? The boundaries we think are uncrossable, the unnameable corners of our soul that we live in fear of bringing to light . . . are the very regions that allow us to feel complete if we dare to explore them. So thank you for crossing borders, shining a light into those corners—they only make you more lovable, more admirable.

I certainly don't quote Peter to suggest that I am more lovable or admirable now but to remind myself of this truth (to paraphrase James Joyce's *Ulysses*): our secrets sit silent in the dark recesses of our hearts, but even they weary of their tyranny, willing and wanting to be dethroned. Stephen Joseph, a professor of psychology at the University of Nottingham and author of *What Doesn't Kill Us*, explains further:

> [A]uthentic people will have deeper and more meaningful relationships with others. Less willing to spend their valuable time in relationships with people who don't care about them, or have their best interests in mind, authentic people seek out relationships in which they can more freely be themselves. You want to be appreciated and valued for who you are, not for who someone else wants you to be. And, in turn, you want to be able to offer the same genuine relationship to others.

Within those messages I received, I especially noted the duads—love and tears alongside joy and release. Yes, I felt unshackled! Yes,

I felt seen! Yes, I felt loved, despite my flaws. And I felt that release—unadulterated joy in being able to be me. More than anything, I'd come to understand how my secrets had prevented me from being known to others, which is to say I had always felt less than my true or authentic self, even in my closest relationships. I allowed others to do precisely the same with me, sharing many of their foibles, failings, and shortcomings. An authentic life, I discovered, led me to authentic joy. Or to turn around the words of Carrie Brown's Ruth just a bit: if you can tell people your true story, then they will know you and you will know them.

## You Do You: How to Live a More Authentic Life

Søren Kierkegaard, who thought a lot about authenticity, referred to the "despair at not willing to be oneself" as a "sickness in the spirit." You can't live an authentic life without having a good sense of who your authentic self is. So we must start by taking an inventory of your core values. These values are formed by your innate personality, your childhood influences, your experiences, and your beliefs. By core values, I mean the things that are most important to *you*—the characteristics and traits you want others to see in you and that drive your behaviors. Here's how to begin.

**Do an online search for "list of core values."** There is no one master list of values, but many studies have been based on social psychologist Shalom Schwartz's theory of basic human values, which started in the 1980s as a list of seven domains (enjoyment, achievement, maturity, self-direction, prosocial, restrictive conformity, and security) and has since been expanded into a complex wheel of values and motivators. These days you will find a wide variety of lists (of the top seven, ten, fifty, or even one hundred). Using any of those lists, search for the values that resonate most and write them down.

**Ask yourself, "What do I value more?"** One way to further home in on what matters to you is to set up some comparisons. For example, is collegiality more important to you than success? (How you answer will have a lot to do with how you react to a fellow employee's promotion at work.) What about honesty or pragmatism? Adventure or safety? Innovation or tradition? Kindness or fairness? Recognizing who you are, which is to say what you believe, will help you make authentic decisions. For me, I'd say that I value honesty over pragmatism, which has led to some thorny situations, especially in my personal relationships. (Yes, sometimes you may want to step out of your comfort zone; in fact, it may be healthy. But understand what and why you're doing so.)

**My authenticity is not yours, and vice versa.** Once you take an honest look at what's important to you, you will have a guide to what constitutes authentic behavior for you. The entire point of striving for authenticity is to be sure it's about you.

**Compare your list with that of a significant other, friend, or family member to help in knowing them better.** One colleague of mine who was struggling with a defiant teen went through an exercise in defining values as part of a family counseling session. When the parental values (honesty, integrity, education, kindness, order, calm) were compared with the teen's (independence, curiosity, success, adventure, experimentation, creativity), it opened a path to respecting differences and allowing everyone to express their own authentic selves.

# THE JOY OF MEMORY

"You should have seen the joy in your face when you opened your present," Julie told me the summer after our mom died. My sister was referring to the velvet box that contained our mother's earrings, which she'd had reset into cuff links for me. Looking at them anew, reincarnated, we both recalled the evening our elegant mother, then in her midfifties, had worn them to the Emmy Awards (the year Dad took home a statuette for a Bill Moyers documentary he had produced). Indeed, Julie and I didn't have to rely on memories alone for that evening; we had a treasured photograph of our father in black tie and our mom in a black cocktail dress, the malachite earrings dangling from her earlobes. (Later, I'd learn that malachite is known as the stone of transformation.)

Much study has been put into the joy of memory, sometimes known as reminiscence therapy, which examines how recalling our past can enhance our well-being. "When an individual recalls a time they successfully coped with adversity, a perception of themselves as being efficacious and able to overcome challenges may be activated and strengthened," researchers from Deakin University recently reported in the journal *Memory*, adding, "The recall of self-defining events that shaped the development of one's identity may increase perceptions of meaning and purpose in life."

Our mother's four-year battle with lung cancer, with my two siblings and me by her side, certainly qualified as a period of adversity. By the time all was said and done, the relationship among the three of us had deepened. I joked that we'd become co-CEOs of our parents, with Jay managing the upkeep of their beach cottage, perilously perched on a cliff overlooking the water; Julie responsible for Mom's day-to-day care; and me in charge of their finances. A friend told me after Mom died, "It's as though the three of you became one organism."

We'd all also grown closer to our mom along the way, taking her for doctor visits, staying overnight in the hospital, and, most importantly, making sure that she got her hair colored and nails painted regularly. No messing around with that! I listened closely to Mom during those appointments, realizing how many stories I didn't know, understanding the great effort she now made to be heard. I also did my level best to listen—really listen—which was, frankly, new to me.

In a compelling essay in the journal *Nursing*, Sandy Klever, a former Veterans Affairs nurse in Iowa City, writes that the key to reminiscence therapy is encouraging people to recall past events—

*happy* times—while talking with a listener in the present. Klever describes one woman whose short-term memory was "shot, but who enjoyed talking about the past." One day that woman confided to Klever, "I like you because you listen to me." Sometimes connection can be that simple.

A different study found that among college students, unearthing memories—whether good or bad—made the students happier, more joyful. "There was a happiness boost from reading and writing all kinds of memories, not just the happy or 'good' memories," write Shriya Sekhsaria and Emily Pronin in "The Unexpected Joy of Memories." Later they discovered much the same when it came to seniors, concluding, "We found that both writing and reading memories made them feel happier. And less lonely!"

Any time I look at that photograph of our parents in our family living room, a door bursts open for me, triggering a cascade of happy memories. Among them, the Christmas break when I'd been accepted into a two-week intensive with the Murray Louis Dance Company, despite my lack of *any* kind of training. On one of those evenings, I came home, still in a black unitard, to show off my interpretation of "a tree in winter," which had garnered much praise because of my "simple and naive" interpretation (according to the dance master himself). Mom roared with laughter that night, her face glowing, although I'm not sure whether she found the unitard or my arborous imitation more humorous. No matter. We'd found a new language, then; a point of connection that stayed with us long after, always leading Mom to laugh out loud when we recalled that story, which we did one last time a few months before her death.

I debuted my new cuff links on the first New Year's Eve after Mom's death, and my first as a single man in nearly two decades. That evening, I very quickly remembered how damn challenging it is to get dressed in formal wear, starting with the cuff link challenge, pushing the posts through both holes of the shirt's cuff (which also heightened the sense of loss I had for my husband). I struggled with posts and hinges—and then the studs, one by one. Finally, success! With my tux and patent leather shoes on (and sporting a silver brooch I'd once given to Mom and that had been returned to me), I walked over to the full-length mirror in my bedroom to review the situation.

Although people usually say I resemble my mother, I first saw my father in the glass—my dad as he'd looked the evening he'd donned his formal wear for the Emmys. I proceeded to hike up my jacket sleeve to reveal the cuff links, which reflected the warm light from the nearby table lamp. In that moment, I saw my mother, her smile frozen in that same photograph, with her earrings aglow from the living room lights of the house I'd grown up in all those years ago. For that moment, we were together again, a family again. A happy family.

My friend Margaret Sartor is a well-known documentary photographer and memoirist, and I talked with her about this photograph of my parents and the joy of memory it both captured and continues to reveal. Margaret and her husband, Alex Harris (also a documentarian), have long photographed each other and their two (now adult) children. "It's simply impossible for me to separate my memories from those pictures," she said, referring to her own family photographs. "They have become our story," she continued, with a trace of her native Louisiana accent still present. "The process, as well as the resulting pictures, has helped all of us to recognize the value of ordinary moments—chaos in the family kitchen, the rituals of hair brushing and bedtime, the morning send-off to school, the backyard birthday party, picking mulberries, playing dress-up, walks with the dog, and so on and so forth. In other words, the pictures are, and have been, a reminder of the small things that make up our larger understanding of who we all are to each other. Because they record not only the details of a face or a place, but also the intimate exchange of a feeling in a particular moment and the trust inherent in the willingness to see and be seen."

Dressed to the nines, I took off to the New Year's Eve celebration, quickly finding myself among a dozen equally bejeweled friends. With a spring roll in one hand, I raised a champagne flute to my lips with the other to purposely reveal one of the cuff links. A few friends paid their compliments, while one demanded playfully, "Tell me about your jewelry!" since I wasn't usually one to wear any adornment. That's when I began to tell the story of the magical conversion of the malachite earrings into my new cuff links, which is really to say, the story of Mom and me and the way our relationship transformed across our lives.

Frankly, I found myself surprised by the power and lucidity of this memory. "It's there," meditation teacher Jeff Warren told me when I recounted this story. "It's been there all along. The idea is that our memories of joy still live inside us, like air pockets." As he explained, the practice is to touch on them again and again: on the bus, on the way to work, or during a quiet moment at home. Re-evoke the experience, re-evoke the feelings. Bring that air pocket of joy back to the surface to treasure.

## How to Practice Finding Joy in Our Memories

Jeff Warren is a Canadian writer and meditation teacher who's genuinely funny, doesn't take himself too seriously, and looks a bit rumpled—like he's just gotten up from a nap—no matter the time of day. He's also vulnerable to a fault, talking one day about his diagnoses of ADHD and bipolar disorder, another about his previous recreational drug use, and then even about his nostril hairs (as a focal point of the breath).

One of my favorite meditations of his is actually titled "The Memory of Joy," which can be found on the Ten Percent Happier app. Jeff describes it as "a guided session on calling to mind a happy memory, to learn about the possibility and development of joy." Bingo! After I'd listened to it a couple of times, I emailed Jeff to ask if we could talk. He agreed.

One of the profound takeaways I had from listening to "The Memory of Joy" was that for the first time, I realized I don't have to be grasping to find joy in the external world—that it actually inhabits me. As Jeff says: "We don't have to wait for joy to come from the outside, but can practice recognizing it on the inside."

I talked with him via Zoom from his Toronto office. On that day, Jeff's visage, bathed in the midday sunlight, reflected both dark and light, which is to say shadow and luminescence. On his wrists are tattoos that read "relaxed" and "awareness," while his right forearm reads "let go."

"How do we start?" I asked.

"You do that simply by remembering a time when you felt joyful."

For many of us, there's a consistency to good memories: a sense of deep connection to people, to place, to specific activities at specific times. To do this practice properly, Jeff said it helps to name the memory because "the act of naming can help bring it into the present moment." In his meditation, he describes giving his own joyful memory a handle—"Market Sunshine"—which transports him to a specific moment in time: "It was a warm day, and I was leaning against the wall of a store, watching people go by. I was happy and had a settled, calm sense of connection and joy. It was wonderful."

I asked Jeff if he would guide me in a short practice. He agreed, so, here we go:

> You can either close your eyes or keep them open. Start by taking a few breaths. Bringing a breath into your belly can help you get more in touch with your body, which is one place where these memories live.
>
> Now bring to mind a moment of joy. It could also be a moment of ease, a time in your life when you felt, "It's good to be alive today. It's good to be this person in this moment, this body, in this world, exactly as it is, right now." For me, this is an honest description of joy. Or maybe it's the company of a particular person, or a special place you go to.

Now describe that place to yourself. What do you remember about the sights and sounds, about the play of light in the trees or shadows on the ground, about the look in people's faces, even the nature or traffic sounds? These little memory clues can help trigger how you felt in your body then and there.

Zero in on that feeling in your body. Try to actually recall what it felt like. Were you warm or cool? How did your skin feel? How did it feel in your throat, in your chest, behind your eyes? How did it feel spatially—behind you, above you, below you, in front of you?

If you had to use a word or a phrase to describe this state of being, what would you choose? Maybe you would describe it as joy, or maybe you would describe it as something else, like openness, or settledness, or peace.

Now link this feeling to the time and place. Some name that will help you remember your memory, help evoke the specific situation—something that captures the memory and the feeling. As you do this, keep steeping in any felt sense of joy, or enjoyment, or ease—any good vibes here right now.

Okay, now open your eyes.

We were done. Jeff asked me if I had connected to a time and place of joy. Indeed, I had.

# THE JOY OF FREUDENFREUDE

I'm not proud to say it, but I have felt more than my share of schadenfreude, the German word for harm (*schaden*) and joy (*freude*), best understood as a gleeful reaction to the failures or misfortunes of others. For example, a friend goes on a once-in-a-lifetime vacation that you can't afford, and then it rains every day. Yes! Or the waiter treats you rudely and then drops his serving tray, which—hello—brings a huge smile to your face.

But these exhilarating moments are shot through with unease, because as satisfying as they may be, they feel so . . . wrong, and antithetical to joy as we know it. Moralists have long despised schadenfreude, with the philosopher Arthur Schopenhauer calling it "an infallible sign of a thoroughly bad heart and profound moral worthlessness." (He also wrote that anyone caught enjoying the suffering of others should be shunned from human society, which puts me on notice.)

I'll admit I've taken a certain measure of delight when a writer garners less than stellar reviews or their sales numbers are lackluster. If there's a silver lining, it's that I'm not alone in harboring such dreadful thoughts. The English novelist William Somerset Maugham apparently thought so, too, reportedly saying on his eighty-fifth birthday, "I realize that for most of us it is not enough to have achieved personal success. One's best friend must also have failed." According to Tiffany Watt Smith, who wrote *Schadenfreude,* it is a global phenomenon. As she writes, "The Japanese have a saying: 'The misfortune of others tastes like honey.' The French speak of *joie maligne*, a diabolical delight in other people's suffering. In Danish it is *skadefryd*; in Hebrew, *simcha la-ed*; in Mandarin, *xìng-zāi-lè-huò*; in Russian, *zloradstvo*; and for the Melanesians who live on the remote Nissan Atoll in Papua New Guinea, it is *banbanam*."

Nor is our joy in others' misfortunes simply a reflection of the current zeitgeist. Smith reports that as far back as two millennia ago, the Romans spoke of *malevolentia*, while even earlier "the Greeks described *epichairekakia* (literally *epi*, over; *chairo*, rejoice; *kakia*, disgrace)." Oh, yes, we humans are quite the disgrace indeed. Not long ago I took a perverse pleasure in reading a study that found soccer fans in Germany were more prone to smile—and smile big—when a rival team missed a penalty than they were when their home team scored. Schadenfreude for the score! The same is true where I live in North Carolina, home of basketball rivals Duke and UNC. My Tar Heel friends take a greater measure of pleasure in Duke's losses than in their own wins. Ditto for the Blue Devils—my alma mater—and their chant, "Go to hell, Carolina!"

"To see others suffer does one good," Friedrich Nietzsche

wrote. "This is a hard saying but an ancient, mighty, human, all-too-human principle." It's even more delicious when shared. I remember experiencing that smidge of joy when someone I've known for many years, a longtime bully who undermined those around her in the workplace, got canned. That day I emailed one word—"Congratulations!"—to a rival of hers, only to receive this quick reply: 💋💋💋💋 Schadenfreude allows us to feel better about ourselves, giving us what social psychologist Richard Smith describes in *The Joy of Pain* as a "downward comparison" of our value vis-à-vis others.

Still, in this matter I must take the side of Teddy Roosevelt, who supposedly once said, "Comparison is the thief of joy." Indeed, schadenfreude is a losing proposition.

Enter freudenfreude, which is the taking of pleasure in someone else's *good* fortune. (Freudenfreude, a newly coined word, is still used more by social scientists than the rest of us, although that's changing.) Freudenfreude goes by several other names, including positive empathy, sympathetic joy, or empathetic happiness. Jud Brewer, a neuroscientist and the director of research and innovation at Brown University's Mindfulness Center, told the *Toronto Star* that "sympathetic joy falls into the category of an experience that's connecting and energizing us." To boot, a small 2021 study looked at the role of positive empathy in our daily lives, finding that it propels acts of kindness, like helping others, and that experiencing empathy boosts our overall sense of well-being.

While reading about this study, I thought back to a few years ago when I'd secured a spot at a writers' residency program in Northern California. These programs tend to be competitive, which can bring out an author's worst tendencies—insecurity, hubris, envy, snobbery, and jealousy. But not this time, not this place. We were three nonfiction authors, living and working together for two weeks at the Mesa Refuge in bucolic Point Reyes Station, California, about sixty minutes north of San Francisco. The view from our rooms—of the estuaries, the flora, the fauna—was nothing less than breathtaking, even during periods of what's known as June Gloom, or the dense morning fog that blankets the coast. Taylor Brorby, then twenty-eight and one of my fellow writers, had arrived from Iowa State University, where he was in the middle of an MFA program. My first take on this lad: earnest. The very definition of a ginger, from his fair skin to his rust-colored hair. Oh, and a talker. I don't recall what Taylor was working on then, but I do remember he worked very hard at it, writing furiously in longhand on his beloved yellow legal pads.

That first evening Taylor took Kate (the third writer in our midst) and me into the kitchen, explaining that he has Type 1 diabetes. As quickly as he finished that sentence, he pulled up his shirt, revealing an insulin pump that he wears 24/7. "Please pay attention to my moods, especially if my usual gregariousness turns taciturn or if I begin to look a little 'glassy.'" For good measure, he added, "I also have a history of seizures." To be honest, I felt like Taylor had asked a lot of us.

Other than our both being writers who are gay men, Taylor and I seemingly had little in common. He'd grown up in a trailer home in rural North Dakota, in a county without a stoplight. His mother worked at the local power plant. I'd grown up in New York City, where my father was a professor and my mother a psychiatric social worker. Taylor struggled mightily as a kid in North Dakota, where it was not okay to be gay. When I came out, my parents sent me to a therapist—a gay therapist. We'd come from two vastly different worlds, with fate having us arrive simultaneously at the doorstep of the Mesa Refuge.

During that week, Taylor confided to me how his aunt had outed him to his entire family, leading him to drop out of Princeton and contemplate suicide. "It was a very dark time for me," he explained in his characteristic North Dakota twang. But Taylor persisted, finding resilience within—a strength that seemed to grow as he earned a master's degree, a college teaching job, and a book contract. His first book, *Boys and Oil,* came out in the late spring of 2022 to stellar reviews. As our friendship developed, I began to understand how his successes—his joys—became acts of resistance and resilience. As Ingrid Fetell Lee, author of *Joyful*, has said, "Rather than being a distraction, when we allow ourselves a moment of joy, it creates a respite that makes us more resilient."

By the end of our two weeks together, I felt such empathy for my friend that I wanted to hug him, protect him. In my mind I became his biggest cheerleader, which wasn't true because he had a squad of cheering friends, including an amazing sister.

Not long ago, Taylor published a guest essay in the opinion pages of *The New York Times*, which is a very big deal for a young writer—heck, for any writer. That day he posted a photo of himself, beaming, holding the print edition. I found myself experiencing such joy in my friend's achievement, and in his evident exuberance. His success lifted me. Sympathetic joy, for sure. I hadn't yet read about freudenfreude, but when I did, I understood it immediately and viscerally. "When we feel happy for others, their joy becomes our joy," wrote Marisa G. Franco, a psychologist and the author of *Platonic.*

On Taylor's social media pages, friends celebrated his successes, taking personal pleasure from them—from him. Freudenfreude, it seems, pushes us to understand an individual's success as a community achievement. "As delicious as it is to delight in our enemy's defeats, celebrating our friends' success—big and small—helps us all triumph in the end," said Catherine Chambliss, a professor of psychology at Ursinus College.

At that point, I recalled the enormously successful 1990s Morrissey song "We Hate It When Our Friends Become Successful," the very definition of schadenfreude. Except that, thanks to my newfound sense of freudenfreude, I'd rewrite that song title just a bit: "We Love It When Our Friends Become Successful."

## Two Ways to Cultivate More Freudenfreude

Knowing that schadenfreude is more common than its nicer cousin, Catherine Chambliss developed a system to help us boost freudenfreude, or what she's described as "the lovely enjoyment of another person's success." In real life this is often not turnkey or instinctive, and so by practicing these exercises, Chambliss says we can learn to be sensitive and supportive of others when they report good news, and deliver the hoped-for "empathetic response of shared joy."

Here are two exercises that Chambliss recommends to get started:

**Shoy**, or sharing joy, involves asking questions of someone who has had a positive experience. Find out more and dig into the other person's happiness. Surprisingly enough, the simple act of engagement and showing interest can rub some of that joy off on you.

**Bragitude** means giving credit to someone else for your success. Had a win at the office? Tell a colleague how they contributed to your promotion. Love the way your garden turned out this year? Mention it to the neighbor who gave you a landscaping idea. Look for ways to reflect your joy back onto someone else, and it can become the gift that keeps on giving.

# THE JOY OF TAKING A PAUSE

Several years ago I was waiting in line at my favorite bake shop, the Bovine Bakery, located about forty-five miles north of San Francisco. The owner, Bridget Devlin, describes it as a "from-scratch bakery," and she's long been a proponent of creating local, organic, and, most of all, "made with love" items. Over three decades I've enjoyed—"scarfed" might be the better word—a wide range of the Bovine's offerings, from the date-almond bran muffins to the chewy chocolate-cherry-almond cookies. But my favorite, hands down, are the scones—especially peach when in season.

On this particular Sunday, a warm June morning, I joined the long line that was already spilling out onto the sidewalk. Awaiting my turn, I chatted with the woman ahead of me, praising the muffins and croissants, but pointedly saying nary a word about the scones, which almost always sell out at some point during the morning rush. I watched several people leave, many of them biting into their still-warm scones. I began to worry.

Finally close to the glass case, I could see that just one beauty remained—its peaches browned perfectly. I could taste the flaky crust. There was only one problem: the woman in between me and "my" scone.

At that moment I heard her tell the barista behind the counter: "I'll have a chocolate croissant." My scone was saved. Joy to the world, or at least to me!

In the next moment, I advanced to the front of the line and pointed to the lone scone. "I'll take that!"

Not one second later, the fellow behind me, a complete stranger, shouted, "That's my scone! I've been waiting in line twenty minutes."

What? I thought to myself. Who is this guy? He's got a lot of nerve to tell me how long he's been in line, when he's actually *behind* me. I heard an entitlement in his voice that provoked me, and frankly echoed my own.

I stood there for what seemed thirty seconds—but what was only a momentary pause—processing this Lycra-clad cycler's proprietary demand for my scone. I didn't claim ownership. I didn't tell him to piss off. Instead, I turned toward him and looked him in the eye and asked, "Would you like half?"

I shocked myself.

What I'd done was simple but long in the works. For several years, one of my meditation teachers repeatedly came back to what she called the "sacred pause"—a breath or two that allows us to choose our next action instead of it choosing us. Without such a pause, our reactions are automatic, instinctive, and unthinking. I'd practiced the pause for a few years, registering a sense of accomplishment after my husband unleashed a fury reminiscent of our Jack Russell terrier, and I remembered to pause rather than retaliate. I'd begun to create a new habit to fall back on when provoked: wait, settle, and speak.

As the Buddhist meditation teacher Jack Kornfield has explained: "In a moment of stopping, we break the spell between past result and automatic reaction. When we pause, we can notice the actual experience, the pain or pleasure, fear or excitement. In the stillness before our habits arise, we become free to act wisely."

Okay, okay, back to the bakery and *that* fellow. I didn't think during my pause, but if I had, I might have asked myself: Is he as hungry as me? Does he love the scones as much as I do? What else might be going on that I don't know about? I remembered a quote I've seen and have reposted on social media from time to time that always gets a ton of likes: "You never know what someone is going through. Be kind. Always."

Once I'd made my offer, I saw befuddlement creep across his face. He took a moment before responding—a pause of his own?—and then accepted my proposal, sweetening the deal. "Why don't I buy another pastry and we can share both of them?"

He did and we did. We sat and talked for about half an hour—he in his cycling Lycra, me in my faded blue jeans. At first blush I'd say we had little in common—from our careers (he a venture capitalist, me a writer), to our ages (Gen Y, Boomer), and political views (traditional Republican, progressive Democrat). But that would be wrong.

As we ate our baked goods, I stopped judging him and found myself actually seeing him. A cyclist, he'd gotten up early to ride some thirty miles to make it to the Bovine Bakery before the morning rush. On this day he'd gotten a flat, making him late.

Not only had we shared a surprising moment of connection; we'd done more than that. We'd recognized each other, and by that I mean we'd seen and heard each other. Instead of saying, "Would you like half?" I might as well have said, "You matter." And vice versa.

Sharing the scone ended up making my day even better than if I'd had it all to myself. What could have been an awful encounter actually ended up leading to a discovery of common ground. I realized that our ability to become vulnerable to each other had allowed us to bridge the social isolation and loneliness that many experts believe fuel mistrust, anger, and polarization, leading us to be withdrawn or rageful.

As it turns out, at the bakery I'd experienced what's known as a helper's high, or what Melanie Rudd, an associate professor of marketing at the University of Houston, calls the boost we get from being kind. Not surprisingly, Rudd told me that once we experience this high—which comes from behaving in a kind or generous manner—we want more of it. As she writes in *Scientific American*, volunteer work is associated with more happiness and less depression. Performing five random acts of kindness on one specific day a week for six weeks can boost your sense of well-being.

Throughout the day, jot down what you did; to derive even more joy, describe how each act made you feel. (Examples include taking out a neighbor's trash, making dinner for a sick friend, or helping a teen with their college essay.)

Research also shows that people who spend money on others experience greater joy. For many years, I tried to inculcate that lesson in two of my ex-husband's young nieces by giving them a cash gift, asking that they spend part of it on each other, and then having them tell me what present they'd given to the other and how that made them feel. One of the girls, a smarty-pants with a big mouth (much like me at that age), decided to make fudge for her sister, which she boasted cost "almost nothing," allowing her to keep most of the cash. Eventually, she came to realize that "time is money," giving me the last laugh, at least that year. Her older sister, meanwhile, gifted a book, exactly the kind of present I'd hoped she'd get for her sister.

Telling people to do good things for others, writes Rudd, appears to be a smart strategy for spreading cheer, care, and connection.

Would anyone like half a scone?

# Peach Buttermilk Scone Recipe from the Bovine Bakery

Bridget Devlin, the bakery's owner, kindly shared her recipe, which she recommends making only when peaches are in season (in other words, no canned peaches).

## PEACH BUTTERMILK SCONE

*This recipe should yield approximately 12 scones.*

### Ingredients

DRY INGREDIENTS

8 cups all-purpose flour

1⅓ cups sugar

⅔ tablespoon baking soda

2 tablespoons baking powder

1 pound butter (cold), cut into cubes

½ tablespoon salt

WET INGREDIENTS

7 eggs

2 tablespoons vanilla

1 cup buttermilk

1 to 2 cups sliced/chopped peaches

## Preparation

1. Preheat oven to 350°F.
2. Sift dry ingredients into a bowl and add cut butter to the mixture, either with a food processor or pastry blade. The end result should have a coarse, pebble-like texture.
3. In a separate bowl, mix together the wet ingredients.
4. Add wet mix to dry mix by hand. Add more buttermilk if needed. The end result should be a raggedy batter, stiff and able to hold its shape.
5. Scoop onto a well-oiled baking sheet or onto parchment paper. Bake at 350°F in the oven for approximately 30 to 40 minutes, or until scone top is golden brown and springs back when touched.
6. Enjoy. And share. (Okay, I added that last bit.)

# THE JOY OF SOLITUDE

After separating from my husband in 2017, after fourteen years of sharing a life and a bed, I moved into a new house and new chapter of my life. Night after night I kept myself busy. I went out to dinner with friends, to the movies, or for a walk with a neighbor. I could not stand to be by myself. It might be more honest to say, I did not *know how* to be by myself.

I remembered my high school read of Thoreau's *Walden*, a book that describes the nineteenth-century essayist's journey to find solitude. "I find it wholesome to be alone the greater part of the time. To be in company, even with the best, is soon wearisome and dissipating. I love to be alone. I never found the companion that was so companionable as solitude."

I longed to find a similar kind of peace—joy, even—in being alone. But I wasn't sure where to begin. Ironically, I began to think that a silent retreat might help me adjust to my post-divorce loneliness.

That's why, in the dead of winter of 2020, I set out on a journey seeking solitude—a silent retreat in the darkest climes of Finland. (I had no way of knowing while making these plans that less than two months later, the world would close its doors and borders.) I imagined the gifts I'd finally find: comfort, solace, serenity—dare I even dream, joy. I took Thoreau's writings and wisdom with me, remembering the powerful impact this sentence had on me in high school: "I went to the woods because I wished to live deliberately, to front only the essential facts of life, and see if I could not learn what it had to teach, and not, when I came to die, discover that I had not lived."

I was no stranger to retreats in general. I had been on yoga retreats, meditation retreats, and even, in 2015, a "tech detox" retreat that meant giving up my phone, iPad, and laptop for three very long days. It certainly wasn't easy to be so cut off from family, friends, and colleagues, with no possibility of a text or phone call. But at least I wasn't completely alone. They may have been strangers to me when I arrived, but at the end of the weekend, my tech-deprived fellow retreaters were practically my soulmates.

Before departing for Finland, I understood that this retreat would offer a different kind of solitude. Though there would be other people on the retreat as well, we would not be allowed to speak to one another. I'd be there for ten days, with heavy snowfall predicted daily and a windchill making it feel like -30°F, during a period when the sun does not rise above the horizon. "January is one of the worst months for going to Lapland," a Nordic meteorological site reported. Nevertheless, I booked my ticket.

At least I could prepare for the weather. I packed my suitcase with state-of-the-art thermal underwear, my shearling-lined L.L.Bean snow boots, a six-hundred-fill-power down jacket (with "a covered placket for wind protection, secured with metal snaps for optimal warmth"), and so much more (including toe and hand warmers).

One of my sisters-in-law, an established meditator, emailed me, "You're so brave to venture into the heart of silence." Honestly, it did not feel that way to me, although soon enough her prophesy became my truth. I had no clue as to how to prepare for both solitude and silence.

On the flight over the dark Atlantic, I jotted on the first page of my journal: "I've been reading about silent retreats for a while now. What is the allure, especially in our modern hyperconnected world?" Then I asked myself the million-dollar question: "What will I find there?" Looking back on this entry, I realize I thought "there" referred to the place, to our group, to everything external. It hadn't occurred to me that "there" might mean inside me.

I'd only begun to meditate in recent months, achieving a daily maximum fifteen or twenty minutes before giving in to discomfort, boredom, hunger—even the sudden need to pee (having just done so before sitting down). I'd given no thought as to what it would mean for my body or my mind to be meditating for at least eleven hours daily.

Twenty-four hours after departing from New York, I arrived in Ivalo, a small town in the Arctic wilderness. Hello, Lapland! Hello, darkness, my new friend!

Upon arrival, our four co-leaders explained that the intent of the retreat was "to disconnect from our usual ways of being, in order to make contact with our inner selves." Leena Pennanen, who runs Finland's Center for Mindfulness, advised kindly, "The goal is not to do but to be." Distractions and diversions are actions—"doing" of some sort, Pennanen said, reminding me of what Jon Kabat-Zinn writes in *Mindfulness for Beginners*: "If we are not careful, it is all too easy to fall into becoming more of a *human doing* than a *human being*, and forget *who* is doing all the doing, and why."

The distinction between "being" and "doing" was lost on me. That very first evening (with talking still permitted), we learned the rules of the retreat: No more speaking to one another. No use of phones or iPads or laptops. No reading. No eye contact with others (not even at meals). No sex (whether solo or with another). And no killing or stealing. (Well, that was a relief, since I've seen many Lifetime made-for-TV movies where the silence of the snow buries all traces of the crime.) This was a strange kind of solitude, physically together in a group but disconnected from one another.

(Disclosure: I was permitted to keep a journal because I had an assignment from *The Washington Post*; otherwise that, too, would have been prohibited.)

Outside the meditation hall, a daily schedule greeted us; it never varied. We'd start at seven a.m., not winding down until nine p.m., with lunch and dinner breaks.

## RETREAT SCHEDULE

| | |
|---|---|
| 7:00 a.m. | Sitting |
| 7:45 a.m. | Breakfast |
| 9:45 a.m. | Sitting |
| 10:30 a.m. | Walking [meditation] |
| 11:00 a.m. | Sitting |
| 11:45 a.m. | Walking |
| 12:15 p.m. | Sitting |
| 12:30 p.m. | Lunch |
| 3:00 p.m. | Sitting |
| 3:30 p.m. | Walking |
| 4:00 p.m. | Sitting |
| 4:45 p.m. | Walking |
| 5:15 p.m. | Sitting |
| 6:00 p.m. | Dinner |
| 8:00 p.m. | Dhamma talk [a lesson about Buddhist principles] |
| 9:00 p.m. | Closing for the day or further practice |

"Who's counting the days?" I scribbled rhetorically in my journal. "Who's counting the number of sits?" When one session ran fifteen minutes longer than I'd expected, I found it "excruciating," writing that evening, "I'm looking for the escape button but also trying to hang on." My mind jumped here and there—to my divorce and its ugliness, to my sister (then undergoing chemotherapy), to deadlines known and unknown. I found myself face-to-face with what one of our co-leaders referred to in our evening talk as "our thousand joys and sorrows." Except, I had yet to be visited by any of the joys.

I feared I was the outlier—the only one who could not sit, who could not shut up, who could not focus—who could not "be." These thoughts preoccupied my mind, giving me something to do, to stew on, to distance me from myself and the rest of the group. In my mind I made a list of other activities I could be doing instead: snowshoeing, visiting the nearby reindeer farm, even hopping on a snowmobile in search of the northern lights. "To do, to do—that is what I want to do," I wrote that evening in my journal. Maybe, I even wondered, could I check the dating apps on my phone (a clear violation of the rules, not to mention a kind of insanity in this desolate wilderness)? "What if 'Leo' is right near me?" I said to myself, going so far as to give my prospective husband a very common Finnish name. In the cold. In the dark. In Lapland. Oh, sure, Steven.

"It takes three days to calm the mind," Pennanen, our co-leader, announced that first evening as I began to see that restlessness, boredom, and discomfort plagued others in our group. My fellow retreaters got up, then sat down. Or lay down. One woman shocked us by speaking out loud to her spouse. A young man turned his chair to face the window (looking into the darkness), with his back to the rest of us. I felt as though he'd given the rest of us the finger. Maybe this is how you do that on a silent retreat?

Pennanen's advice proved right, as she'd led many silent retreats previously. On the third day we had a small group check-in, where eight of us could talk together—yes, talk!—for thirty whole minutes. I spoke up first, confessing to my "struggle of detaching" from the world. One by one the others piled on: "I'm exhausted from doing nothing—nothing!" "I am so unsettled." "My life is unmanageable." "Too much stress, too much fear of living in these times." And "too much pain of loneliness." A mother broke down in tears, missing her son. A scientist told us, "I fear for the planet."

"For many of us," Bob Stahl, another of our leaders, explained that evening during his dhamma talk, "it's not easy to be inside our skin, muscle, connective tissue, bones, bone marrow, and being."

"So much for the joy of solitude," I wrote down later that evening, having heard the tale of a novice meditator who'd fled from her "meditation prison" early on. I, too, wanted to flee. The difference? She'd been at a retreat center in Great Barrington, Massachusetts, where you can hop on a Greyhound bus or call for an Uber, not in the Arctic, where you are stuck.

"We are frankly a beautiful collection of frayed and wobbly human beings," I continued that evening, adding, to my surprise, "Connection made." A transformation had begun. We started to get to know each other through gestures like placing a hand over the heart as a greeting, waving someone ahead through a door, even tapping a new friend on the shoulder to point out that a show of the northern lights had just begun. The silence persisted, but the solitude had begun to dissolve. I'd found ways to bridge worlds, even without words.

I volunteered to make the coffee every morning, which meant getting up thirty minutes before everyone else and walking alone through the blowing snow, about a quarter mile, to the meditation hall. I had made myself useful—useful in service to others. Almost as beneficial, I felt the gratitude from my fellow coffee drinkers, who thanked me with namaste bows, reminding me of what Booker T. Washington once said: "Those who are happiest are those who do the most for others."

By week's end, I felt both settled and unhurried. I wrote:

> I am inhabiting moments—actually more than moments—minutes, fifteen or twenty minutes, even more—of this contented quiet peace. The external world is silent—except for the plows and the crunch of boots on the snow and the wind, always the wind—as I have journeyed inward to a new terrain, a landscape that is vast and quiet. There's a peacefulness to it, a balance, an energy field—but not one that causes overheating or disruption. Everything is just buzzing along. I actually feel like my real self—the self I remember before needing to take an anti-anxiety medication. I also feel a heightened sense of focus and energy—and lightness and community. . . .

To my utter surprise, I felt connected to this group of twenty, to whom I'd said practically nothing. I had learned how to "be" with them, and, more importantly, with myself. No doing required.

After our final meditation, I wrote in my journal: "At long last, it's begun. I feel alive."

My newfound sense of ease with solitude was sorely tested two months later when the lockdown began. Of course, this kind of retreat was very different; for starters, it was not voluntary. And it arrived at a time when so many of us were already experiencing a profound sense of disconnection and polarization. We were already in the depths of what U.S. Surgeon General Vivek Murthy would declare in 2023 was an "epidemic of loneliness."

In the fall of 2021, pretty much at the midpoint of the pandemic, I gave a talk on the social media site Meetup about combatting loneliness and isolation. I'll admit I was shocked when 2,500 people joined the one-hour conversation in the middle of a workday. The hundreds of questions had a handful of themes, including how to make friends in a time when socializing had become dangerous to our health, how to find meaning in life after retirement, and most basically, how to connect with others.

I knew from my retreat experience in Finland (which, curiously, had been essential preparation for the Covid lockdown) that we can always find new ways to feel connected to one another. We don't need to be in the same room; we don't even need to speak.

As Julianne Holt-Lunstad, a professor of psychology and neuroscience at Brigham Young University, told me, "Someone may be lonely but not isolated, or they may be isolated but not lonely." Her perspective on this helped me to shift mine, which I shared during that Meetup talk.

I guess I was luckier than most at the outset of the pandemic-induced solitude, having so recently learned the lessons of my retreat. The lockdown followed a pattern I recognized from that trip—a sudden, cold-turkey sense of isolation, filled with dread and silence. Then, gradually, as the time ticked by, I learned how to find what Jeremy Nobel, a Harvard physician and the president of the Foundation for Art and Healing, refers to as "authentic connection." That starts with being connected to ourselves, knowing what matters to us, and knowing those we care about. It morphs into dropping our facades, showing vulnerability, and sharing our true feelings.

Instead of silent namaste bows, I exchanged smiles and waves with neighbors from a safe distance. I wasn't making coffee for fellow retreaters, but at Thanksgiving that year I made several batches of pumpkin-chocolate-chip muffins (a signature item of mine) and distributed them to neighbors. I took out people's trash; when I found a jackpot supply of toilet paper, I bought extra and handed it out (remember, TP was in shortage early in the pandemic). I increased my volunteer time. A neighbor of mine, a textile artist, printed one hundred calendars and left them all over town on our doorsteps. And although Zoom was no substitute for being with friends and colleagues in person, it certainly helped fill the well of loneliness that solitude can create. Being locked down or shut in did not necessarily mean disconnected or isolated.

I found sparks of joy in all that. Then, a new puppy came to live with me. In the early days, Mr. Binx tore up the newspaper, plucked my (dirty) underwear from the laundry basket, and began his lifelong pursuit of the squirrels, chipmunks, and one really big hedgehog. He was a riot on four legs; his joy overflowed and proved contagious (reminding me that not all contagions are deadly).

With the pandemic now (mostly) in our rearview mirror, I think back on both the retreat and the early lockdown as teaching me new ways to cultivate connection, and the importance of solitude in allowing us to savor it. Howard Axelrod, a friend and author of *The Point of Vanishing,* deepened my appreciation for the benefits of being alone.

"Attention becomes remarkably easy," he began on one of our phone calls. "There is great joy in having that level of attention. I think that's part of why people go on vacation—because the worries of their life can be put on hold. They don't have daily demands, and they're often astonished by how beautiful the sky is where they are, or the buildings, or whatever. A big part of why they're experiencing that beauty is that their attention has changed. They're open to receiving what's around them in a very different way. I had that kind of joy every morning when I walked out of the house to snowshoe or to walk up into the woods, as I made my tea, as I made the fire. . . . It's impossible not to feel alive, not to feel grateful for being alive in a place like that. I think that's a kind of ecstasy—a kind of quiet ecstasy."

## How to Find Solitude

Make no mistake, I'm glad the pandemic lockdowns are over. I would never again want to go through months of solitary confinement. But there is real beauty and peace in being alone or quiet, a state of grace often out of our reach thanks to our hyperconnected lives. To find solitude, I'm not going to recommend locking yourself in an isolation booth for a week. But how about finding some time to be alone and off your devices, creating time for thought and reflection, and space to unwind (maybe even create), all of which can help you appreciate and experience so much of what gets lost in the daily grind. Here are a few easy and free ways to establish solitude time:

**Get away.** Leave the AirPods and cell phones at home and venture out, whether in a big city or a small town. Walk on your town's greenway or take a hike. Plop yourself down on a park bench or find a shady tree to sit under. You can even close your office or bedroom door (but do let people know what you're doing and why).

**Take a bath.** If you haven't sunk into a warm tub since you were a child, you don't know what you're missing. It is one of the most comforting, soothing experiences you can give yourself, and (most of the time, anyway) it's a lovely solo experience. Bubbles optional.

**Meditate.** There are many forms of meditation, and many phone apps to guide you through getting started. Some of my favorites include Ten Percent Happier, Calm, and Headspace. Whether you're concentrating on your breath, repeating a mantra, or listening to the recorded sounds of nature, you will be alone in your own head.

**Read a book.** A printed one, with pages that you turn instead of screens that you scroll through. It's not quite the same as being alone with your own thoughts, but it's an escape into someone else's world—alone.

I know, I know, you don't have time to carve out an hour a day for yourself. Start with ten minutes once a week and prioritize it. Work your way up to every day. Then push it to, say, fifteen minutes a day.

**Extra credit:** Find one entire day for solitude—yes, really, a whole day—without social media, news headlines, or texts. If you live alone, you can lock the door, turn off the phone, and focus on yourself, or you can go somewhere for the day entirely by yourself. If your home is overflowing with others (and yes, I know sometimes even one other person can overfill a house!), then either send them all out for the day or book yourself a day trip somewhere.

# THE JOY OF COOKING

Let me say this kindly but directly: my mother was not a great cook. To boot, she took no joy in cooking. The other moms in our mostly Jewish neighborhood relied on manuals like *The Settlement Cook Book* as well as their mothers' recipes, often handwritten on three-by-five index cards, to dish it up. They cooked from scratch, and I loved being invited to Shabbat dinners of brisket and kasha. As my friend Peter Stein remembered, meals made by his German Jewish grandmother weren't just about what was served on the plate. They embodied his family's survival through history. Each dish was a link to a long lineage of German Jewish grandmothers before her.

My mom had no such culinary history. Her mother, born in New York City, relied on a cook to make the family's meals, and we often heard that Grandma Marjorie couldn't even make a plate of scrambled eggs (although she could make a perfect Manhattan). Similarly, Mom's go-to advice book wasn't even in the kitchen but could be found on her bedside table—Betty Friedan's *The Feminine Mystique*—with its silent but powerful warning: the cook is out.

Mom became known as Shake 'n Bake for her signature supper, which she served along with Rice-A-Roni ("the San Francisco Treat") and Le Sueur ("premium canned") peas. For a special indulgence, Mom would defrost one of our family's few culinary traditions, Sara Lee Classic Iced Chocolate Brownies, a dessert that my grandmother loved and loved to give us, elegantly served on her bone china (which first passed to my mom and now lives in my kitchen cabinets).

As a teen, I'd shown more aptitude than Mom in the kitchen, perfecting a recipe for lyonnaise potatoes (or as I called them, "pommes de terre sautées à la lyonnaise," showing off my high school French). They were basically white potatoes, boiled and then sliced and shallow fried, served together with fried onions. More than anything, Mom appreciated that I'd cook them for the whole family, almost every Sunday.

When the time came for me to head to college in the fall of 1974, Mom sent me off with Irma S. Rombauer's *Joy of Cooking*, which then boasted more than four thousand recipes and a joie de vivre not found in other cookbooks. Like most parents, Mom wanted better for me—and for her by extension. "Please come home with new recipes to share," she wrote me that October. (As I was living in a dorm and on the meal plan, I don't know what Mom expected but, for sure, I didn't deliver.)

That first winter away from home, I began to suffer from what turned out to be major depression. The Gothic-style Duke campus, coupled with weeks of rain, left me lethargic and sullen. I didn't understand what was happening, but I recall symptoms like a bad flu (minus a temperature or cough). I felt poisoned. I was scared, which led me to make an appointment at Student Health to speak with a psychiatrist who asked me little but quickly scribbled a prescription for five-milligram Valium tabs and told me, "Take one, two to four times a day." Alas, those yellow tablets did little to lift my mood and much to dull my senses. Before the end of my first year, I'd convinced the therapist to make a case to the dean that would allow me to move off campus, explaining that the heavy emphasis on drinking and the social pressure to date women in the dorms had taken a toll. "I also want to be able to cook for myself," I'd told him, describing it as a form of self-care long before that phrase came into currency.

By year two, I had a room of my own and a kitchen. My copy of *Joy of Cooking* sat proudly on the Formica counter, and I began to experiment with different recipes—banana bread, Country Captain Chicken (a fragrant curried chicken dish), and lasagna—practicing what later became known as food as medicine. Soon enough I became more than proficient at *Joy*'s roast chicken, boasting of it as "my signature dinner," a humblebrag that implied expertise in more than one recipe. (Well, I could still make those lyonnaise potatoes!)

Back then I knew nothing about Irma Rombauer, the creator of *Joy of Cooking*. In time I learned how the cookbook was born out of tragedy.

Two months after the stock market crash in October 1929, Edgar Rombauer, Irma's husband of thirty-one years, died of a self-inflicted gunshot wound. He was known to have suffered from depression, leaving Irma a widow and a social outcast thanks to the stigma associated with suicide. With her two "kids" then adults in their twenties, Rombauer, who had long relied on servants to prepare the family's meals, sought something to do and decided that Depression-era home cooks needed a plain-speaking cookbook more geared to the zeitgeist of that era. "Assume nothing, teach everything and most importantly find the joy" became Rombauer's mission, according to one of her biographers, as she embarked on creating the book that came to be known as *Joy of Cooking,* a title that surely defied the grief she was experiencing.

(Rombauer had taken half of her $6,000 inheritance and self-published three thousand copies of the book a year after Edgar's death. Nine decades later, and never out of print, *Joy of Cooking* boasts cumulative sales of more than twenty million, making it one of America's top-selling cookbooks of all time.)

Rombauer's daughter, Marion, later acknowledged that her mother wrote the cookbook "chiefly to distract her keen unhappiness." Meanwhile, a food historian also took note of Rombauer's circumstances, writing, "What made *Joy of Cooking* really catch on was its timing—luck in an era of deep loss and struggle."

By the time Irma Rombauer died in 1962, at age eighty-four, her *Joy of Cooking* had become a mainstay in American kitchens. She was eulogized as a woman who "made one of the ordinary and daily necessities of life into something more than ordinary. She gave many persons, often deadened by drudgery and dullness, a vision of the manner in which the ordinary could be transformed into an act of beauty and an achievement for the human spirit. . . ." The minister concluded that by being in her presence, which he explained even came through on the page, our lives were "transformed" and "exalted," "lifted up one level higher."

I know what that minister meant. On most Sundays when still in college, I invited a couple, maybe three, friends over to my place for supper. I'd spend the week planning a simple menu from *Joy of Cooking*, sometimes attempting a new recipe, other times replicating the tried and true. I found that feeding friends filled my heart as much as it did their stomachs. It brought them to my table, and I loved this act of giving, which in turn helped me to feel useful in a practical and meaningful way, reminding me of what Mark Twain once wrote: "To get the full value of a joy you must have somebody to divide it with." Although it's a bit of a leap, I can see now that one era's Great Depression served to stabilize my chronic depression.

Subsequent research into what is now often referred to as culinary therapy has only bolstered what I—and so many others—knew already. Home cooking is linked with heightened relaxation, greater awareness, boosted confidence, and yes, joy. In the early 2000s, Michael Kocet, then professor and chair of the Department of Counselor Education at Bridgewater State University in Massachusetts, started taking cooking classes in the evening. "When I would tell people . . . they would say, 'Oh, cooking is so therapeutic for me,'" he said. This eventually led him to teach a course on culinary therapy to counseling and psychology students, and to develop a study looking at cooking and baking as mitigating factors for stress and anxiety. Kocet shared with me that food often plays a powerful role in family relationships and special occasions—like births, birthdays, celebrations, weddings, funerals, and religious observances. "Food and cooking can help facilitate healthy communication among families and individuals, and can help in dealing with conflict and painful issues that exist in individuals, groups, and families," Kocet explained. He added that "culinary or cooking therapy can be a potentially effective intervention that can enable people to examine deeply painful emotional/psychological issues in a meaningful way that touches at the core of their familial history with food."

In the years since Kocet's realization, study after study has reported that our ability to cook is positively linked with stronger family ties, lessened feelings of isolation, better mental health, and lower levels of depression. A psychology researcher agreed, reporting that cooking and baking are associated with better emotional functioning, which she calls "flourishing."

In time I came to see myself as a descendant of the Irma Rombauer school of cooking, and I only need point to one of my greatest life triumphs—perfecting *Joy of Cooking*'s pecan pie recipe. I made my first attempt while still an undergrad in North Carolina. In those early years, I religiously followed Rombauer's recipe, creaming the butter with a cup of firmly packed brown sugar, beating in three eggs one at a time, and then stirring in light corn syrup, broken pecans, and a teaspoon of vanilla. A few decades later I have made it my own.

Ever since my first pecan pie came out of the oven a toasty caramel, I became my family's "pecan pie king." The competition surely wasn't much. Mom—who took even less joy in baking than she did in cooking—still bought her holiday pies at the A&P. I trounced her, easy-peasy. No matter where we celebrated Christmas, everyone knew Steven brought the pecan pie.

For years I sat on the holiday pie throne without fear of challenge, learning early what my Tar Heel neighbor Frances Mayes writes in *Under the Tuscan Sun*: "[P]ecan pie [is] a necessary ingredient of Christmas." The longevity of my reign, I thought, was the result of the time and innovation I brought to making my pies. Over the years, I had tinkered with Irma Rombauer's recipe, making a few crucial changes: a generous helping of Kentucky bourbon (instead of the vanilla extract) to cut the treacly sweetness of the dark Karo syrup (no more light syrup), the use of fresh whole pecans (instead of chopped nuts of an unknown vintage), and a top-secret mixing technique that prevents my pies from becoming gelatinous.

Perfection! If I say so myself.

Over the years my pies saw us through our family's ups and downs—including the deaths of my grandmother and my parents, my divorce, the births of three nieces and a nephew, as well as my cyclical depression. Standing in the kitchen while beating the eggs, measuring the Karo syrup, culling the pecans, and melting the butter grounded me in the present. In a world of change, these pies are a touchstone, a constant.

Each pie is also a memory, and then a memory of a memory, reminding me of the petite madeleines in Marcel Proust's *Remembrance of Things Past*. On a frigid winter day, Proust's narrator returns home, where his mother is serving tea and those little cakes.

> And soon, mechanically, weary after a dismal day with the prospect of a depressing morrow, I raised to my lips a spoonful of the tea in which I had soaked a morsel of the madeleine. No sooner had the warm liquid, mixed with the crumbs of the cake, touched my palate than a shudder ran through my whole body, and I stopped, intent on the extraordinary changes that were taking place in me. An exquisite pleasure had invaded my senses, but individual, detached, with no suggestion of its origin. At once the

> vicissitudes of life had become indifferent to me, its disasters innocuous, its brevity illusory. . . . I had ceased to feel mediocre, contingent, mortal. Whence could it have come to me, this all-powerful joy?*

Over the succeeding forty years I've defended my pie title against newcomers, like Megan, a sister-in-law who brought her own pecan pie to our holiday table, now a long time ago. When she announced her contribution, I felt betrayed by my family, who had allowed this to happen. Megan, beautiful and blond as well as eight and a half months pregnant that November, had my people in her hands, especially when she launched into a long story about how her heirloom pecans came from her godmother's farm in Lamar, Missouri. "Every year she handpicks them, hand shells them, and then sends them to me. The magic of her pecans is part of what makes this pie so delicious!" By the time she was finished, I knew I was finished. No matter how delicious my pie, no matter how sweet my pecans, Megan's family tale was about to trump mine, with my very own flesh and blood ready to dethrone me, which they did with Karo syrup glistening on their lips.

By the following year I had created my own—true—pie origin story, which opened with my gathering of the pecans from a mom-and-pop farm in Goldsboro, North Carolina. This was my first holiday with my new husband's family, and I wanted to make a

*From Marcel Proust, *Swann's Way, In Search of Lost Time, Volume 1: The C. K. Scott Moncrieff Translation,* edited and annotated by William C. Carter (New Haven: Yale University Press, 2013).

good impression. The tale was Rabelais's *Gargantua and Pantagruel* all over again, and I told it slowly and carefully: famine, floods, and pestilence! I included online testimonials from others about my farm-to-pie-tin nuts, like this over-the-top one: "I'll buy them every year until death do us part!" I also mixed in my own family story as a way of introducing myself to the new in-laws. By dessert's end, the voting was in. My pie pan was empty. Half of the other pecan pie—made with a chocolate graham cracker crust and maple, instead of Karo, syrup—remained in its tin pan.

As for what I've learned in my forty years of pie making, well, I've actually come to see that it's not about the bourbon or my secret mixing technique. It's not about whether you use Karo or maple syrup, a traditional or chocolate bottom crust, or the pedigree of the nuts. It's about the life of the pie—the joyful traditions we mix up year after year that, with any luck, bind us together as family. That is also the real message of *Joy of Cooking*, which Irma Rombauer knew instinctively, as she held her family—and millions of readers—together in the churning wake of troubled times.

I'd add that my view of my mom's Shake 'n Bake dinners also evolved during those years, notably that her way of cooking brought her joy in its own way—even if from a box. At her memorial service, stories about her faux Southern-fried chicken dinners continued to spur joy among those who'd eaten at her table, and envy among those who had not been so lucky.

# Steven Petrow's Bourbon Pecan Pie as Featured in *The New York Times*

## Ingredients

1 cup dark Karo syrup

1 cup white sugar

3 eggs

2 tablespoons unsalted butter, melted

¼ cup bourbon (you can use as little as 2 tablespoons if you prefer)

1 teaspoon almond extract

1½ to 1¾ cups (about 6 to 7 ounces) whole pecans (the best and freshest you can find; learn as much about them as you can, whether from the farmer or the label)

1 unbaked 9-inch-deep piecrust

## Preparation

1. Preheat oven to 350°F.
2. Combine the Karo syrup, sugar, eggs, melted butter, bourbon, and almond extract. Mix well.

3. Fold in the pecans, making sure they're evenly distributed throughout the filling. Do not overmix.

4. Pour filling into the unbaked piecrust. With your fingers, arrange the topmost layer of pecans so they are lying flat with the rounded side facing up (no need to become too obsessive).

5. Bake for 55 to 60 minutes, until a toothpick inserted in the center comes out clean.

6. Let the pie cool for at least two hours.

# THE JOY OF GETTING LOST

When I was in graduate school back in the mid-1980s, I made a new friend, a fellow volunteer on my regular shift at the San Francisco AIDS Foundation hotline. Kurt, like me, always answered the phone with the standard script: "Hello, I'm __________, a hotline volunteer. How can I help you today?"

What we heard in return were voices filled with panic and terror:

> "I have many gay friends. Can straight people get AIDS?"
>
> "I just learned that I'm HIV positive—is this a death sentence?"
>
> "I have a purple lesion. Do you think it's Kaposi sarcoma?" (One of the cancers associated with HIV/AIDS.)

We felt a huge responsibility in answering these callers—not just for providing up-to-date and accurate information related to their queries, but for being attentive to their usually frayed emotional states. We had to be present, one hundred percent present.

We also learned how AIDS Foundation volunteers and staff tended to come and go. I don't mean that they'd leave for vacations (which they did) or find new job opportunities (which they did), but that they'd die. Suddenly. One week they'd be with us—Meredith, Chuck, Ron, Tom, Ken, Ernesto, Joe, and another Joe—and the next week we'd see their "in memoriam" photos on the wall or in the pages-long obituary section of the *Bay Area Reporter.*

One afternoon, a year after we'd begun volunteering, Kurt turned to me and said, "Let's get lost." I wasn't sure what he meant. Did he want to go out for a beer after our shift? Was he simply ready to leave for the day, now, having hit a wall? Or was it a play on Chet Baker's iconic song ("Let's Get Lost")? As it turned out, he meant it literally.

"Let's find a time to get in the car, drive and drive, until we get lost. No destination. We'll stop when we get hungry." I answered, "Sure," not voicing much enthusiasm. He tried to gin me up. "I've done this before, you'll see."

A few days later I pulled up to Kurt's flat near Golden Gate Park in my VW Beetle. We were off! To somewhere, nowhere. Shrouded in fog, San Francisco looked ethereal in my rearview mirror as we drove over the Bay Bridge toward Oakland. Kurt explained that he'd be directing me when to turn, but that he wasn't the "navigator" because that would imply he knew where we were going. "Sure," I answered, again, game but still less than enthused.

Once off the Bay Bridge, we stayed on I-80 as the mighty interstate took a northward swing. We passed by Berkeley and then a row of East Bay towns whose names I knew but no more than that: El Sobrante, Pinole, and Hercules. Then Kurt directed me off the freeway. Every couple of miles I'd hear, "Take this left," "Go straight here," "Let's make a right." We did this for an hour or so.

"Sometimes getting lost is a good thing, as it forces us to be more aware of our surroundings," I'd read in a book of travel essays. Indeed, at each juncture—left, right, or straight ahead—I'd paid close attention to a gas station, a church, even a historic hotel, thinking of them as breadcrumbs, to make sure we could find our way home. (Remember this was long before the age of GPS and cell phones.) These markers quickly appeared and then disappeared, one by one, from the rearview mirror as we continued on our way—to nowhere.

"Do you know where we are?" I finally asked.

"Nope," Kurt said, with a look of contentment on his face.

"You mean we're lost?"

"Yup!" Kurt replied excitedly.

If life were as perfect as it is in a Disney movie, I'd tell you that we wound up in an open field blanketed by wildflowers. Or on a coastal overlook, where we watched the whales breach. But no such luck. All of our turns had taken us to a dead end, leaving us at what appeared to be a scene from a Mad Max movie.

From the car, Kurt and I looked out over a postapocalyptic wasteland containing what appeared to be an endless maze of pipes, chimney stacks, steel columns, and round containers (painted in various pastel hues). Smoke billowed from several of the chimneys, some of it white, but much of it black. This sprawling industrial complex showed no sign of life, at least from our vantage point. A sulfurous odor engulfed us.

It didn't take long before I realized we'd driven to the massive oil refinery near Martinez, a plant known for its repeated violations of environmental and safety codes, which in later years resulted in two catastrophic and fatal accidents.

You might think our experiment had failed us, having delivered us to such a toxic site. Actually not. Here, where nothing was familiar, I felt untethered from the life and places I knew. That entailed a certain kind of freedom, or joyousness, which is just what Kurt had hoped we might discover.

By now ravenous, we took lunch at a small café just outside the gates of the refinery where we sat on the porch and ate ham-and-cheese sandwiches on white bread. While eating, we watched the smoke rise, staining the sky. Although we'd only traveled about forty miles, we were elsewhere, having left behind—if only for a few hours—our day-to-day lives. I know it makes little sense to say that our fleeting whereabouts—that industrial wasteland—comforted us, but it did. For a little while, we weren't witnessing our friends, ravaged by this still-new plague, walking uneasily up Castro Street, their faces gaunt, their backsides stained by loose stools. We didn't hear the ambulances rushing to San Francisco

General Hospital, carrying our colleagues who could not breathe, or had lost consciousness. We were not at a celebration of life, or what we'd better know as a memorial service.

Once done with our lunch, Kurt and I drove back directly, passing by the gas station, church, and the hotel that I'd noted earlier as landmarks. We took the freeway back over the Bay Bridge and into the city, where I deposited him at his front door. I experienced a sense of rapture—"a feeling of intense pleasure or joy"—at the day's unfolding. For years, Kurt and I referred to "our adventure in getting lost" as the foundation of our friendship, and as a small antidote to the encompassing darkness of that time.

Years after Kurt's and my adventure, Rebecca Solnit wrote an entire book about just this, *A Field Guide to Getting Lost*, which speaks to the joy of wandering the unknown. Notably, she focuses on what we can learn about ourselves in the process.

> To lose yourself: a voluptuous surrender, lost in your arms, lost to the world, utterly immersed in what is present so that its surroundings fade away. . . . [T]o be lost is to be fully present, and to be fully present is to be capable of being in uncertainty and mystery. And one does not get lost

but loses oneself, with the implication that it is a conscious choice, a chosen surrender, a psychic state achievable through geography.

That thing the nature of which is totally unknown to you is usually what you need to find, and finding it is a matter of getting lost.

Thank you, Kurt, for teaching me why we get lost.

## How to Get Lost

It's so much harder to get lost these days than when I went on my adventure with Kurt. In our phones there are street-level maps of where we live and work; actually, pretty much the entire globe is mapped these days. (When I was on retreat in northernmost Finland, above the Arctic Circle, I turned on MapQuest and could see exactly where I was thanks to Wi-Fi, Bluetooth, GPS, and cellular location features.) We need to make a conscious decision to get lost, but that doesn't necessarily mean "missing" or "stranded," or in any way unfindable. So, how do we get lost on purpose, which is really another way to ask, how do we find new experiences and people off the well-trodden paths?

(I'll preface this suggestion by saying that of course you should never put yourself in danger, so don't set off on a hike into an unknown wilderness without a *printed* map, for example, or take a walk, especially alone, in an unfamiliar area.)

The hardest part of this adventure is giving yourself permission to wander—to make it, as the saying goes, not about the destination, but about the journey. (Although I'd add to this, make it about the company you take along with you.) It's also about shifting your mindset to embrace the heart of travel, which is exploring. You may decide to plan this day out or do it spontaneously, although I'd be sure to tell a friend what you're up to, what direction you're heading, and when you plan to be back.

A friend of mine recently found herself with an unplanned day to spend in a West Coast city where she'd never been. She described it to me as "unsettling, yet energizing, to be in a totally unfamiliar place." Walking downtown streets with unfamiliar names, looking up at snow-capped mountains in the distance, and talking with locals, my friend found moments of serendipity and discovery that we don't experience much of anymore.

So here's your assignment: Pick a town, even a neighborhood, you've never visited, and go there without a plan. Don't look up the tourist attractions, don't research restaurants, don't plot out a self-guided walking tour. Just go. Walk around. Ask for directions at a gas station or from someone walking their dog. Look at menus in restaurant windows instead of scouring Yelp reviews. When you get home, write down what you did, what you experienced, and how that was different than a planned excursion.

Now, get lost!

# THE JOY OF YOUR NAME

As a newspaper columnist, I'm applauded by many of my readers—and, frankly, not so liked by others. That's the name of the game, and in an age of doxxing and trolling, I get a lot of heat. I've often said that I appreciate hearing from those who disagree with me, although less so if their messages are weighed down by curse words and other vitriol.

Surprisingly, many of these people email from their personal accounts—do they think they're anonymous?—which gives me the opportunity to respond. My intent is not to change their hearts and minds, but to establish some kind of connection, even civil discourse, which in this day and age should be reason to shout with joy. To do that, I've learned it's crucial to start by addressing each other by name.

I learned the importance of this type of personal exchange a few years ago. Like many writers, I'd set up an autoreply to acknowledge receipt of each email: "Due to the high volume of email I receive, I may not reply to you, but know that I've received your message." What I came to realize is that many interpreted that response as saying, "I'm too busy and too important to acknowledge you and your message properly." I didn't understand how off-putting my response was, or how invisible and unheard it made letter writers feel. I get it now—thanks to the notorious Westboro Baptist Church and X, formerly Twitter, of all things.

In 2016 I listened to a TED Talk by Megan Phelps-Roper, the granddaughter of the late reverend Fred Phelps Sr., who founded Westboro Baptist. A 2007 BBC documentary referred to the Phelps clan as "the most hated family in America." You may have seen members holding up those "God Hates Fags" signs as they picketed military funerals, claiming that service members were being killed because of our nation's acceptance of LGBTQ+ rights. In her talk, Phelps-Roper described standing in a picket line on a Kansas street as a blue-eyed, chubby-cheeked five-year-old, "my fists clutching a sign that I couldn't read yet." "Gays Are Worthy of Death," shouted the placard in her hands.

By the time she reached her twenties, Phelps-Roper decided she'd had enough of the hatred. She stopped picketing and effectively divorced her family. In her TED Talk, she explained that she owed her transformation to, of all things, Twitter. Complete strangers who took umbrage at Westboro Baptist's picketing sent her messages filled with "rage and scorn," as she put it. Instead of replying in kind, she began to answer them with cute smiley faces, pop culture references, and Bible verses. "They would be understandably confused and caught off guard, but then a conversation would ensue," she said. "And it was civil—full of genuine curiosity on both sides."

Most importantly, explained Phelps-Roper, "We'd started to see each other as human beings, and it changed the way we spoke to one another." As those conversations continued—deeply and respectfully, and by name instead of name-calling—she began to rethink her positions, and ultimately decided to leave the church, and her family, behind.

Not long after I'd listened to her talk, I began my own experiment with readers who had a beef with me. Instead of ignoring them with my one-size-fits-all autoreply, I'd write them back, addressing each personally, by name. Here's one example, which served as my template:

> Dear Bill,
>
> Thank you for taking the time to write me. I am actually a person, and not a bot. I am at my desk and have read your email. Honestly, I can tell that you're angry with my perspective but I can't tell why. It's hard for me to get past the name-calling. Could you write back and explain why you disagree with me? Thank you.

I signed each email "Steven."

About two-thirds of those I emailed replied, and they started off by acknowledging their shock that a living, breathing human being had taken the time to read their words and respond individually. Most apologized for their foul language, name-calling, whatever the infraction had been. From there, they'd get into the substance of their disagreement with me—whether the topic was same-sex marriage, climate change, or our forty-fifth president. Now we were talking! I didn't try to persuade anyone that I was right, only that it was important to be able to talk about hot-button political issues. I discovered, like Phelps-Roper, that my antagonists "didn't abandon their beliefs or principles—only their scorn." Even better, I sometimes saw my attempts at kindness or humor reflected back toward me. Whoa. We were experiencing real-life empathy in real time.

Polarization in our country deepened during the pandemic, as did our collective loneliness. I experienced it myself, witnessing it pretty much everywhere, among teens and seniors, teachers and students, singles and marrieds. In all those Zoom meetings and webinars, I saw us in our cages—I mean our little Zoom boxes—never to hug or make eye contact.

Midway through the pandemic, I began to take an online class with John Gaydos, a longtime yoga instructor in Los Angeles, who began each session by greeting us individually—even though there were often close to a hundred students. I especially liked his own twist on these introductions, as he'd say, "Saying hello to . . . Steven." Hey, that's me! I thought each and every time. And then he'd proceed to say hello to the next person, who no longer seemed to be locked in a box. They'd smile, or wave, or reply, "Hi, John."

A fellow student, Michelle Solotar, told me she found his greetings "sweet and charming," but Gaydos explained to me just how "instinctive" or intentional he meant them to be. He said that he had no idea what the students would make of his personalized greeting, but he hoped we'd feel welcomed and cared for. "How could I walk into a room or show up online with no acknowledgment of my presence?" he continued. "Greeting them also makes it more real for me." Indeed, you could always hear the chorus of "Hi, John!" replies.

I loved it. It spoke to me. He spoke to me. During this strange and isolated time, when so many of us felt disconnected, invisible, Gaydos connected us. He saw us. Hanh Kihara, another student, told me that Gaydos's personal greetings "created a sense of community."

Kihara continued. "The hellos and goodbyes reminded me of all the invisible yogis who shared the same joys of the practice and feelings of well-being." Solotar found even greater meaning in his welcoming ways. As she told me, "I've had the lifelong experience of being unseen and, as bad or worse, unremembered." Now in midlife, she recalls her younger, more socially active days, when "I was so invisible to others that I frequently questioned my own existence."

A 2023 Gallup poll found that adults in the United States who regularly say hello to six other people in their neighborhood experience greater well-being than those who greet fewer. According to the poll, "Americans' well-being score increases steadily by the number of neighbors greeted, from 51.5 among those saying hello to zero neighbors to 64.1 for those greeting six neighbors." That's roughly a 30 percent boost—simply by saying hello. Call me crazy, but that seems to be an awfully easy fix.

I've learned that calling a person by their name can also boost how we feel, even more so, of course, when it's their correct name. Michelle, my fellow student in Gaydos's class, told me she has often been referred to as any one of many "M" names, from Marsha and Melanie to Melinda and Melissa. Whenever I introduce myself as Steven, I immediately brace for the reply, which is often either "Steve" or "Pete," the latter a confusion with Petrow, which means "son of Peter" in Ukrainian.

When someone gets my name right—or even better, remembers it the next time we meet—that makes me feel important, valued, and seen. Food writer Angelo Pellegrini, in his 1948 book, *The Unprejudiced Palate*, wrote about "the significance latent in little things." Among those little things, he suggests, are our names. You show respect in calling an individual by their name; conversely you display disrespect in not asking or forgetting. I also have found that it helps build bonds between individuals and strengthens our relationships, which allows for being seen and heard, all building blocks for experiencing joy.

This is where I'd usually include an expert's opinion to buttress or qualify my perspective. In this case, I'm giving a shout-out to Blue Summit Supplies, an office supply store based in Huntsville, Alabama, that features a blog post on its website about why we should try to learn and remember names. "Our name represents our identity as well as our personal history, family background, and connection to our culture and community," suggests the writer. "The power of names is deeply personal, which means hearing our own name can have a profound psychological effect." And by that they mean a powerful, positive one.

As it turns out, research has shown that "there is unique brain activation specific to one's own name in relation to the names of others." This takes place in the left hemisphere, including the middle frontal cortex, middle and superior temporal cortex, and cuneus. Put more colloquially, hearing your own name sets off a chemical reaction inside your brain, releasing so-called feel-good hormones like dopamine and serotonin, which increase our experience of joy as well as trust, empathy, and compassion.

This shouldn't come as a surprise—many of us have seen the joy of new parents calling their baby by the name they've chosen, the thrill of a newlywed using a new married name for the first time, or the validation of a transgender individual claiming their new identity. It really is among the sweetest and most important sounds we hear.

## Create Joy for Someone: Use Their Name

If you're like me, you often forget a person's name the minute after they are introduced. Also like me, you have probably read plenty of those tips and tricks for remembering someone's name (ask them to repeat it for you; use it right away; or associate it with something else, like Ruby with very red lips).

My challenge for you now is to use an introduction as the opportunity to create some joy in the person you've just met. Try this the next time you are introduced to someone—at work, at a party, anywhere. I'll make a bet that not only will you remember their name, but you'll spark and spread a moment of joy. While I'm gazing into my crystal ball, I predict that that person will remember your name, too.

**Repeat the name when it's said first.** Of course, this is always at the top of any "how to remember names" list. Someone says to you, "This is Jackie"; you immediately say, "So nice to meet you, Jackie."

**Engage the person on the meaning of their name.** "What a lovely name. Is it short for Jacqueline?" or "My best friend in high school was named Jackie—I'll never forget the fun we had!" Or even "Like Jaclyn Smith? She was my favorite on *Charlie's Angels*!" (For now, skip worrying about how to spell Jackie, or is it Jacquie, Jacque, or even Jacqui?)

**Make note of how hearing their own name affects them, and respond to that**. They may have a story to tell about how they were named for a relative, or about how their parents disagreed about the unusual spelling of the name. (My parents did not agree on my name until I was three months old, and my birth certificate is proof; it reads "Baby Male Petrow." My mother argued for "Christopher," my dad for "Mike." After all that, who could forget it's "Steven"?) If your gesture of using their name or listening to a personal anecdote brings them a little joy, you've done a fine thing.

# THE JOY OF SOLIDARITY

A few weeks before Thanksgiving a couple of years ago, my friend and fellow journalist Steven Overly, then thirty-three, woke up on vacation in Palm Springs, California, with what he's described as a "cacophony of a dozen dial-up modems blaring inside my head." Confused and alarmed, he called out to a friend in the next room and realized he could barely hear his own voice, although he was apparently shouting. When his friend responded, the words sounded muffled. As Steven told me on the phone, "I had simply gone to sleep with my hearing intact, and come morning it was gone."

Steven's life had changed, perhaps forever.

Once home in Washington, D.C., Steven, olive complected with a full beard and an appealingly crooked smile, spent months shuffling from one specialist to another, undergoing a wide range of tests and treatments that included an MRI and a CT scan, oral steroids, liquid steroids injected into his eardrums, and electrodes stuck to his face. With no definitive diagnosis, he started wearing hearing aids and learning American Sign Language. Eventually he was diagnosed with Ménière's disease, a disorder caused by a buildup of fluid in the inner ear that can lead to symptoms such as vertigo, nausea, vomiting, loss of hearing, ringing in the ears, headaches, and loss of balance.

As Steven adapted to using hearing devices, he worried about the impact that the loss of his hearing could have on his career as a journalist. What he couldn't appreciate at the time was how his identity would also morph, as he began to think of himself as "hearing impaired," which allowed for an unexpected opportunity: solidarity with a new community.

I'd call this "the joy of togetherness," which we certainly realized we needed during the pandemic, when families could not share birthdays, holidays, weddings, graduations, even rites like funerals together. Paul Born, who wrote *Deepening Community*, notes that the most important benefit of community is "feeling a sense of belonging." He continues in an essay, "To belong is to be cared for and to reciprocate that caring, to know that 'I am home.' It is a willingness to extend our identity to a group of people or to an experience."

Chris M. Meadows, a clinical psychologist and psychotherapist, was long considered one of the preeminent scholars on joy, having conducted a large study of "joyful experience" in the 1970s. He detailed that 70 percent of the reported joyful experiences were what he called "affiliative"—that is, joy shared with others. His research reinforced the notion that joy is typically social, whether as part of a club, school affiliation, or professional organization, or as a result of belonging to an identity group (like groups based on race or ethnicity, gender, sexual identity, or disability).

I was actually surprised to read that people in general—even those who describe themselves as loners or introverts—claim to be happier and more joyful when they are around others than when they are on their own. Ruth Whippman, author of *America the Anxious*, wrote in an op-ed, "Study after study shows that good social relationships are the strongest, most consistent predictor there is of a happy life. . . . This is a finding that cuts across race, age, gender, income and social class so overwhelmingly that it dwarfs any other factor."

Steven wasn't just concerned about whether he could continue to do his job (and whether his employer might question his ability to do the job). Recently single, he also worried about the impact on his dating life, especially in loud clubs and bars. Could he still travel safely overseas—one of his greatest joys? As he told me, "I was having a difficult time dealing with the change, dealing with the emotions, and more than anything, not knowing whether there was going to be an end to it."

Steven had to confront the idea that he was now considered, as he put it, "disabled," which left him feeling "increasingly vulnerable and very alone." As he told me, "I was navigating the uncertainty of not only a new medical condition but also a new sense of self."

Roughly a year after his illness began, Steven texted me, asking for advice about the pros and cons of writing a personal essay about how hearing loss had impacted his life. By this time, we'd been friends for six years; we'd met at a journalism convention and begun a conversation that turned into dinner with other colleagues. Since then our friendship has only deepened. Steven knew I often wrote first-person essays about some of the medical challenges I've faced—including depression, sexual dysfunction, and my fear of a cancer recurrence. Each time I'd written a column, I'd found unexpected but very welcome support from readers who shared my experiences (and my fears). For instance, when I acknowledged living with lifelong depression in the pages of *The New York Times* in 2016, I was astounded by the consideration of readers, many of whom wrote as one man did: "You are not at all alone."

Not long before Steven reached out to me, I'd also found a surprising sense of solidarity with a group I hadn't even known existed. I'd written a column for *The Washington Post* about how I began to shoplift as a reaction to my sister's increasingly dire cancer prognosis. For many obvious reasons, this column had been difficult for me to write. First, I had to acknowledge to myself what I'd been doing. I felt highly vulnerable by allowing myself to be open about these repeated, and let's face it, illegal episodes.

What would people think of me? Would I jeopardize this book contract? Would I be arrested?

My shoplifting had begun spontaneously when Julie, a participant in a highly experimental cancer clinical trial, developed new and painful symptoms each week the drug was administered. One week we thought she might be having a heart attack. Another time, we worried that she'd go blind from the overflow of mucus in her eyes. How many more side effects could she endure? One gray morning while visiting Julie, who had been hospitalized because of the unpredictability and severity of the side effects, I found myself completely overwhelmed at seeing my sister in such pain and decided to take a short break. I left her room and took the elevator down to the gift shop, where I picked up a newspaper and poured myself a cup of coffee. No one was at the register. After patiently waiting a couple of minutes, I suddenly and uncharacteristically became consumed with rage at the nonexistent service. My rage quickly extended beyond the gift shop to the doctor who had downplayed the new drug's side effects. Then to my fear that Julie might die. Not to forget a laundry list of life grievances that I'd never fully expressed. All of a sudden, years if not decades of anger consumed me. Talk about a perfect storm. There I was at the gift shop, with no clerk present to take my money. "F*** this, f*** them," I said out loud—but to no one—and walked out with the *Times* under my arm and a coffee in hand. I felt empowered, like I was "giving it to the man." I did this three days in a row; I didn't get caught. The cost of my total theft: $16.50, which hardly diminished my rage.

Two weeks later, still angry and confused about Julie's health,

I "forgot" to pay for the $25 salad bowl I'd placed on the lower rack of a supermarket shopping cart, sailing through the self-checkout station. What was going on with me? I didn't understand, except to say that I felt possessed. No matter, I continued to shoplift.

I'll end this part of the narrative by saying I confessed to several friends, who didn't judge me but urged me to get professional help, which I did. I had to laugh when I asked my friend Ed Chaney, an attorney, for legal advice. His reply: "You need a better therapist." In time I did stop, notably as Julie's condition improved (albeit temporarily). I called the manager of each store I'd stolen from, asking how to make restitution. That was the best I knew how to do. Then I wrote a column about it.

While I hadn't expected anyone to pat me on the back, I was taken aback by how unkind and aggressive some readers were to me. Many of their posts could be summed up like this one: "Lock him up."

But alongside these comments were others by readers who shared their own shoplifting incidents. For sure, it's one thing to know that one out of eleven Americans, or nearly twenty-five million individuals, shoplift each year, according to the National Association for Shoplifting Prevention. It's another to read people's stories, tied to mine, and to feel a connection with them.

> "I really felt the author's panic and discomfort when hearing each of his sister's bad reports. I can also completely understand the momentary rush of distracting excitement and the feeling that you've gotten some kind of justice, and that you've evened the score somehow by snatching the item

(however small and trivial) back from the dark monster that's trying to take everything from you."

"This urge strikes me more often than I'd like to admit. Instead of me beating myself up for even imagining such a thing, now I'll see it as a symptom of some other mental turbulence."

"Several years ago, a friend of mine who was going through a terrible divorce confided to me that he'd stolen a pair of cuff links from his father, with whom he was staying. I remember feeling baffled by that act, but this article puts it into some context: an irrational but compelling response to unbearable stress and sadness."

But here's what completely surprised me: the sense of solidarity or belonging that resulted, and the satisfaction I derived by feeling the embrace of these strangers. Frankly, I felt something close to elation at reading how many people understood me (even when I still struggled to do so), and at knowing that many of them extended me kindness and a measure of grace (even though I'd yet to do so fully for myself).

"Solidarity," I'll admit, might at first seem like a peculiar word choice here. I usually think of solidarity when it comes to political protests, as in, "Factory workers voiced solidarity with the striking students." In that context, I understand the sense of belonging that can result.

But as it turns out, solidarity doesn't require a political affiliation—it can be found in any shared experience that creates a sense of kinship. The pandemic certainly offered its share of those. Iona Brannon writes about one example in an essay in *Bon Appétit* called "This Online Group Taught Me the Joy and Solidarity of Buying Nothing." Brannon had just moved into a new neighborhood in Los Angeles when the pandemic hit and she was furloughed from her job. Home alone all day, she began joining different Facebook groups, "longing for some sense of community," which is how she found the Buy Nothing group. She got involved and began walking around her new neighborhood to pick up or deliver items to neighbors she hadn't even met.

"During pickups, I saw their front yards, their herb gardens, their handwritten scribbles on paper bags. I used their homegrown spring onions in my salad, their passion fruit in my smoothies, and their sourdough starter in my bread. It's a strange sort of intimacy: I felt like I knew these people even though we hadn't met face-to-face."

Her poignant essay reminded me of what the Very Reverend Bill Terry, the now-retired pastor of St. Anna's Episcopal Church in New Orleans, had written in *Ambush* magazine: "Sharing the joy and sharing the struggle SOLIDARITY!" Amen.

I encouraged Steven Overly to write about his experiences, which he did several months later in a beautiful column published in *The New York Times*. The response was overwhelmingly positive; in the first twenty-four hours, Steven received more than five hundred personal messages. "I had the validation that people either identified with my experience or felt a greater understanding because of my experience," he told me on the phone, using Bluetooth that connects to his hearing aids. "The volume and the content of the responses was just very, very moving, very overwhelming, and very thrilling in a lot of ways."

I asked if he would share some of the responses that had the greatest meaning to him, which he graciously did. One message was from an individual with significant hearing loss who acknowledged feeling completely overwhelmed, and who wrote, "But now I know that I am not alone, and that these feelings are real and justified. I don't know if our paths will ever cross in person, but I wanted you to know how much you have given me by sharing your pain."

Another woman had a completely different health issue but connected with his essay. "I have recently encountered health problems that have created a 'before and after' moment in my life, too, about which I have yet to feel pride, though perhaps that will come with time. From your writing . . . I can see a path forward that includes not only accepting my limitations, but finding value and community that are sustaining."

Many of those who corresponded with Steven had no medical issues but still found common ground with him, which gave me a dollop of hope about our ability to empathize with those we don't know. "I hope that I'm not alone when I say that your words have opened my mind about how to appreciate other people's difficulties and to be grateful every day for the many things I take for granted," one individual wrote in an email. "Wishing you healing, grace and peace."

At this point in our conversation, Steven suddenly returned to a question about joy and vulnerability I'd asked him right after his essay was published, connecting it to these moving responses. I could hear the excitement in his voice as he explained, "I found an unexpected joy in feeling a sense of purpose in what I had done, that making myself vulnerable and sharing this experience has actually helped people in a very direct way. . . . We often hear that in abstract terms, like, 'Oh, sharing your story helps others.' It's not that I didn't believe it was true, but I had never experienced it myself. I did feel like people were helped by me sharing my story, and that gave me a greater sense of purpose. I definitely felt some joy in that."

I asked if any other aspects of joy had come his way as a result, and he took off like my cocker spaniel chasing a squirrel. "There's a sense of joy from the solidarity and the validation I felt from sharing my experience; from having other people identify with your hardships and knowing that you're not alone in them. I don't feel any joy from the fact that other people are going through this terrible experience, but I do feel less alone and I do feel better understood because of it."

Both in his *Times* essay and our conversation, Steven threaded the story of his new identity as a member of the disabled community with his personal story of coming out as gay. He recalled a moment on the dance floor of a queer club in Washington, D.C., with Beyoncé's *Renaissance* in full throttle, when he became aware of how central community has been to his gay identity—and how absent it has been from his new one. "My sexual orientation has become a source of positive self-definition in my life in large part because of the bonds I've formed with people like me, people who are now friends and mentors and have shaped my sensibilities and values." He added that before coming out he constantly worried about being outed, or doing something that would out himself. "When you come out you're able to dispel all of that. It doesn't mean you don't still face challenges. It doesn't mean there aren't situations where you feel vulnerable. But you're able to trade one set of vulnerabilities for another. What I'm finding with both coming out as gay and with sharing my hearing loss experience is that I would rather face the vulnerabilities that come with being honest and being open and not feeling any sense of shame about who you are than continuing to face the vulnerabilities that come with being dishonest, closed off, and insecure."

Solidarity, indeed! I know I've gained strength and developed new friendships and connections by choosing to be open and vulnerable about my many issues and peccadilloes. I'm also reminded of what the Dalai Lama has said about just this: "The real source of inner joy is to remain truthful and honest." Without meaning to one-up His Holiness, I'd argue that the real source of inner joy is to *become* truthful and honest, like Steven Overly.

## How to Find Kinship with Others

I remember how shocking it was more than twenty years ago to read *Bowling Alone,* Robert Putnam's account of how disconnected we'd then become. It's not an exaggeration to say I found the book devastating, as he points out the decline in club memberships, civic associations, PTAs, churches, political clubs, and sports leagues—leading to a "disintegration" of community and social structures. The drop in voter participation (from nearly 63 percent in 1960 to less than 50 percent in 1996) was another disheartening trend that showed a decreasing interest in civic life.

For many of us, the disintegration of community life happened so gradually that we didn't notice—at least not until Putnam's book came out. All, however, was not lost. That edition ended on a hopeful note, as he reminded us that civic reinvention had happened before and could happen again. Little did he know then how the Internet, still in its infancy when he was writing his book, would multiply our collective and individual sense of disconnection. As Melissa Hughes, a TEDx speaker and writer, blogged, "The irony of the 'connectedness' that platforms like Facebook, Twitter, TikTok, and Instagram proffer is that we're more disconnected and lonely than ever."

Now our challenge—and your assignment—is to document examples of solidarity with others, identify strengths and weaknesses in that list, and find ways to create kinship. You know I love a list, so get out pen and paper or pick up your phone and get started. Create three lists:

### LIST #1: WHAT COMMUNITIES DO I FEEL CONNECTED TO?

Include in this list everything from medical conditions to sports allegiances and anything in between. What about your identity do you share with others? Your list may include your nationality, race, ethnicity, gender, or sexual orientation. It may also include your favorite musician, a love of theater or books, or the fact that you grew up in Brooklyn. There can be many, many items on this list.

### LIST #2: WHAT COMMUNITIES HAVE I ALREADY JOINED?

I'll bet this list is a lot shorter. Do you belong to an online patient community, a local book club, a professional organization? Don't include social media pages that you simply follow—I'm talking about groups in which you have truly engaged with others. Give yourself a pat on the back for these, as you are connecting in ways that too few people do.

### LIST #3: WHAT COMMUNITIES WOULD I FIND JOY IN JOINING?

These are your opportunities. Different from your first two lists, this one will be rich with ideas for how to better connect. Do you have strong political beliefs but lack active political participation? Love to read but never joined a book club? Been lurking in an online group for years but never posted anything? This is your entry into twenty-first-century connections. Now you have a road map of how to find communities that will matter to you.

It doesn't count unless you write it down, so begin your challenge . . . now!

# THE JOY OF BLUE

Back in the spring of 1983, a time when I was studying day in and day out for my Ph.D. oral exams at Berkeley, rarely sleeping, and fraught with anxiety, a good friend suggested I take a day trip to Stinson Beach, a seaside village in Marin County just north of San Francisco. "It has healing properties and will calm you," she insisted, adding that the town's potency came from the rolling surf of the Pacific Ocean. "There's also a great burger shack, right on the beach," she added, in case I hadn't been sold by her mystical assertions.

Three days later I hopped into my old Beetle and headed across the Richmond–San Rafael Bridge, admiring the expansive view of San Francisco Bay below, and its pointillism of different blues. I felt both calmer and, weirdly, more energized, two responses researchers often associate with water.

Thirty minutes later, my car and I crested on Highway 1, a narrow cliff road that often falls victim to one natural disaster or another—from mudslides and asphalt fractures to high winds and wildfires.

With the road now falling away in many places—pay attention!—the entire expanse of Stinson Beach was revealed, the blue waters of the Pacific framing the white sand. It was both terrifying and a tonic.

It took me but minutes to descend to the village, with its (then) year-round population of just over seven hundred folks. I left my Bug in the official parking lot and trudged over a small dune, when suddenly I was greeted by the sea. (Further afield I could see a half dozen surfers bobbing in the water, awaiting the next swell.) I remember being blinded by the sun, breathing in the salty air, and listening to the surf roll in. It was a lot, all at once.

In my backpack I had a ham-and-cheese sandwich, a bottle of water, and Anne Morrow Lindbergh's beautiful memoir *Gift from the Sea*, which had been a gift from my friend Mimi, also in the doctoral program. I ate my lunch and took a short nap, and then opened the slender book, turning by chance to this short passage: "Patience, patience, patience, is what the sea teaches. Patience and faith. One should lie empty, open, choiceless as a beach—waiting for a gift from the sea."

I was not a man who knew patience, much less faith. Instead, I got up, dusted the sand off my legs and butt, and jogged easily from one end of the crescent cove to the other—and back—about six miles altogether, as happy memories of growing up on a different beach, by a different sea, mixed in with those now being made.

A year after that first trek to Stinson Beach, I was diagnosed with testicular cancer. The year, 1984. My age, twenty-six. The surgery, eight hours long. While I was still recovering in the hospital, a biofeedback therapist had come to my room, asking a straightforward enough question: "Where do you see yourself going to heal?"

Even though my parents wanted to take care of me in their New York City apartment, with its view of a gas station on Houston Street, I returned to the West Coast, where I had a small pool in the backyard, and to Stinson Beach six weeks later.

Two months ago, I flew out West to make my pilgrimage to Stinson Beach for the thirty-eighth time (having missed but one year due to Covid). This year as I sat on the warm sand, looking out to the horizon, the waves rolling in, the sandpipers frolicking, I experienced the patience, openness, and sense of wonder that Anne Morrow Lindbergh described so many years ago. Yes, I felt small against this backdrop, but not insignificant. I felt like this was where I belonged.

Only in recent years, thanks to marine biologist Wallace J. Nichols, have I begun to understand the science underlying our connection to the sea. Nichols, author of *Blue Mind,* is one of the world's leading experts on the healing power of water and, more to my interests, how water brings us joy.

In his book, Nichols writes about the proven health benefits of water, such as reducing stress and anxiety, lowering heart and breathing rates, and notably, increasing our overall sense of well-being and joyousness. He explained to me that the "blue mind" refers to a "mildly meditative state," one that occurs when we're near, in, or under water, in any of its many forms. Naturally skeptical, I asked him to define what he meant by a "mildly meditative state," and he quickly recited a list of "C" words: "calm, creative, coherent, compassionate, connected to ourselves and each other and the water itself."

"The color blue has been found by an overwhelming amount of people to be associated with feelings of calm and peace," wrote Richard Shuster, Psy.D., a clinical psychologist. "Staring at the ocean actually changes our brain waves' frequency and puts us into a mild meditative state," he added, using the same language as Nichols. Other researchers report that cooling sea breezes provide their own health benefits, which leads me to wonder if that's why so many English novelists sent characters away for a "sea cure."

Curious, I asked Nichols if we need literally to be at the ocean to reap benefits, to which he emphatically replied, "No." After all, not everyone has the same access to oceans or lakes. Nichols understands this, which is partly why one of his first questions to someone new is either "What's your water?" or "What's the water you first fell in love with?" Over the years he's heard many answers. For some people, it's what Nichols refers to as "wild" water: lakes and rivers; creeks and ponds; rain, snow, and ice; and, of course, the ocean. For others, it's "domestic" water: swimming pools and hot tubs, water tanks and bathtubs, even the water in a sink, garden hose, or sprinkler. Nichols also points out urban water features in cities large and small: fountains in public plazas and parks ("urban" water). Wow—water, water, everywhere. "Most people can walk to some wild or urban water, wherever they are in the world," he told me.

About that point in our conversation, I remember wondering, What's joy got to do with this? Or, put another way, Where's the joy? I asked Nichols to talk about the role of water in helping us cultivate joy, specifically in terms of *eudaimonia*, Greek for "the pleasure of living and doing well," which is considered one of the primary definitions of joy. "When I think of joy, I think of surprise, pleasant surprise, a playfulness," Nichols began. "Water and play go together so well. For instance, when I talk about play and water, often I'll say, 'Balloons are fun. But water balloons are a real party. Slides are great but waterslides are just more joyful, and in surprising ways. There's the big splash at the end, there's slipping around, and it's just the next level.' Parks are cool, water parks are next level. You have all the joy in the play and the surprise aspect."

Nichols had one more point to make, this one about how memories can be connected to nostalgia. By that, he explained, "So many people have such beautiful, rich, important moments, with people that they love, that involve water." As he spoke those words, I instantly remembered joyful times with my siblings at the ocean as kids (bodysurfing and building sandcastles), and even more recently kayaking on a long and winding river not far from my house in the Blue Ridge Mountains. "The lasting joy comes from remembering the event, the time spent in that place of joy, and then being able to conjure it up, as needed, later," said Nichols.

I hadn't really thought about this before, but Nichols is on to something when he says water-related memories remain so clear because they exclude much of the background noise. He explained that "when you're in the water, you're probably not holding an iPad or [watching] a wide-screen TV. There aren't a lot of billboards [to distract], nor a lot of traffic noise. Generally speaking, the water does some work in reducing the other kinds of sensory input that are just always present—although a very crowded pool can certainly be noisy."

I thought about this for a while and realized that only the day before, I'd taken a short hike in the woods with my iPhone in hand the entire time, both to take photos and check texts. I realized I hadn't been fully aware of my surroundings, which sure makes it hard to create memories. "The water sets you up for that mildly meditative place with limited distractions," Nichols continued, worrying aloud about Apple's latest efforts to make its phones waterproof.

I think all this explains why it is that, for nearly four decades now, Stinson is where I go to heal, to celebrate, and to express my gratitude in a quest to be whole. Each year when I reach the breach between Stinson Beach and its neighboring town to the north, Bolinas, I lie down on my back, feeling my body sink into the sand, feeling at one with the elements. On those good days when there's no fog, I also feel the warmth of the sun on my face, and thanks to the heat of the sand, I imagine a direct connection with the earth's core. This is where I belong. This is home.

## Finding Your Blue

I've been fortunate enough to live near "wild" water for most of my life, and I know well the healing power of going to land's end—whether the ocean, a lake, or a stream. Of course, not everyone lives by a body of water, or can travel to the beach on a regular basis. More and more of us live in parched deserts, without a lake or pond in sight. (Thank you, climate change.) No matter, you can still find your blue.

**Start local.** Do an online map search for nearby lakes and ponds, looking for blue spaces. You may be surprised to find that a park you've never visited has a small body of water in it. Recently, a friend told me that after a decade in her neighborhood, she discovered that the playground where her kids used the swings and slides had a lake at the other end of the park. Who knew? Even urban fountains and koi ponds can provide the same benefit. Explore!

**Expand your search.** You may not live by open water, but look for creeks or rivers within easy driving distance of home; in fact, more and more parks are accessible using public transit. A walk along a riverside trail listening to water rushing over rocks, or watching a cascading waterfall, can be soulful medicine.

**Plan your next vacation around water.** Think about incorporating water into an upcoming trip. Find some blue and make it your destination. Again, it need not be the Atlantic, the Pacific, or the Caribbean. I start many mornings walking around a small reservoir called Trout Lake in the Blue Ridge Mountains of North Carolina. (Point of information: it's not a lake and there aren't any trout in it—only bass. Whatever!) If you set an intention, you'll likely find it.

Finally, there's always the home version of a blue water experience. Take a bath or shower and relax into the warmth.

# THE JOY OF WRITING BY HAND

I wasn't happy when major credit card companies announced a few years ago that signatures would no longer be required to make a purchase. With the stroke of a virtual pen, American Express, Discover, Mastercard, and Visa erased the need to provide even our laziest, often illegible, but always most telling identifying feature. Yes, I understood that in an all-digital world our John Hancocks are hardly the security equivalent of Face ID or two-factor authentication. Still, since online banking had become the norm, I'd already given up—and missed—signing checks. I had loved to take my pen of choice in hand, usually an inexpensive gel point, and then with a flourish affix my unique (and illegible) signature on a check for a niece's birthday or a donation to a favorite nonprofit. To "write a check" these days is as impersonal as three clicks plus typing in the amount.

With those headlines, I thought back to a handwriting experiment I conducted years ago. Curious to see if I could recognize my friends' penmanship, I asked four male friends to send me a postcard, each with the same greeting: "Having a wonderful time. Wish you were here." (They weren't allowed to choose a postcard that revealed where they lived, which would have invalidated my little experiment.)

These pals included a real estate agent, an architect, a fellow journalist, and an actor (who should be more aptly called an adult entertainer). As the postcards arrived in my letter box, I'll admit I could not identify a single one of my correspondents by their penmanship. How sad, although I did peg Aaron, the adult entertainer, as the architect, a bit of foreshadowing as several years later he joined an architecture firm—as a landscaper—which, perhaps, meant I'd seen his essence even before he had.

Handwriting, once one of the most instantly identifiable elements of an individual, has been lost to the ages, trampled into dust under the relentless advance of keyboards, touch screens, and voice recognition software. "Whether we write in print, cursive, or a combination of both, our handwriting is much more than a vehicle for communication," Cortnee Howard, a CNN contributor, writes. "It is a visual representation of our personality: of who we are, what we've learned and who we want to be." Philip Hensher, author of *The Missing Ink*, agrees, writing, "In the past, handwriting has been regarded as almost the most powerful sign of our individuality. . . . [I]t has been seen as the unknowing key to our souls and our innermost nature."

Hensher believes that our handwriting styles are windows into our souls, claiming, for example, that "people who don't join up their letters are often creative [or] they may be a little bit slow." (Make up your mind, sir.) Another hypothesis of his: "People who don't close up their lower-case g's are very bad at keeping secrets," which he admits is also a challenge for him, prompting him to reflect, "If I took to closing my g's scrupulously, would I start to be able to keep other people's secrets?" I don't know if all of Hensher's suppositions are valid, but his main premise certainly is.

Handwriting remains fascinating, even as it's fast becoming obsolete. Fifteen years ago, I found myself taking a stand against a couple I know well who had traded away hand-signed printed cards in favor of digital ones with no signature, not even a handwritten XO or ♥. "It's so impersonal you might as well do nothing," I vented. The following year, to my delight, I found a hand-signed paper card in my mailbox. It's not that I wanted them to put in more effort (okay, I did want that), but holiday cards still tell our stories, which requires a connection to time and place.

I feel like an outlier, but at least Hensher is with me (or I'm with him). I'm also with journalist Damon Beres, who writes that "getting [cards] in the mail is like receiving a wee present before Christmas—and that opening an *email*, for crying out loud, is hardly the same as digging your thumb into an overly spit-wet envelope from your grandparents with a picture of them nestled next to a fireplace buried within like cardboard treasure." Indeed.

I'd add that the card sender is also the beneficiary of a gift. There's a ritual in putting pen to paper (as there is in choosing pen and paper) that pushes the mind and the hand to slow down. For sure, I don't want to mess up and have to make a correction in ink—or worse, hunt down my vintage bottle of Wite-Out and start all over again. I write deliberately, sometimes making a trial run in my notebook. There are all sorts of studies showing that the process of writing by hand, rather than tapping on a device, ignites greater brain activity, cognitive understanding, and creativity. Raymond Walters, a British artist who died in 2020, has said he always wrote with "purpose and intent, and waited for the reply. To me, it encourages a more deliberate way of living."

Put another way, writing by hand gives us the time to feel and decide how to express ourselves. Some people have even higher standards, disdaining routine writing implements. Shekar Mahalingam, an entrepreneur studying psychology, writes in his essay "The Joy of Writing," how penning a letter "seemed a drudgery done with a lifeless ballpoint pen" or, even more to the point, "bereft of joy." How he longed "for [his] bountiful fountain pen," its reservoir "filled to the brim with feelings of endearment, joy and sorrow." I'm not nearly as poetic as Mahalingam, nor do I need a quill pen to express myself, but I do like seeing how quirky my scrawl is, how it reflects my temperament on any given day, and how it provides tangible evidence of my imperfections—and passions. I'm not sure my handwriting is an opening into my soul, but it is revealing of who I am, which definitely allows others to know me better.

Remember my friend Taylor Brorby, the author? He writes all first drafts by hand, explaining, "I love my handwriting and I like seeing it, rather than picking out some standard font on a computer. Writing by hand helps me know that I am me first and foremost . . . There's something so private and personal working in hard copy." I've actually seen Taylor's hard-copy texts and they're works of art. Black ink on a yellow legal pad, his distinctive penmanship is what he describes as "an odd combination of print and cursive." Unlike his computer—where music by Lizzo, the history of the Grand Duchy of Tuscany, or his medical bills are only a click away—the only thing on those legal pads is Taylor's writing, which he says "brings me so much joy." His handwriting has also brought joy to his many friends, as he's constantly writing cards and notes—to everyone, that is, except his grandmother, who pronounces his cursive "horrible."

Speaking of grandmothers, I've long treasured letters from my mother's mom, in part because I know her beautiful script took time and concentration to execute. At the upper left of each envelope, Grandma would write out her full name, Marjorie L. Straus, relying on the Palmer Method of penmanship, a style that incorporates distinctive curlicues, especially evident in the "M," "L," and "S" within her name. (To this day, Palmer style remains the gold standard when it comes to what "good" handwriting looks like.)

As a kid (even before I could read), I recognized those flourishes, equating them with Grandma. Now as I file and organize the dozens of cards and notes she sent to me during her lifetime, I realize all are signed exactly the same way: "Love, Grandma." The "L" and the "G" are original to her hand, to her identity.

Grandma Marjorie died in 1973, when I was sixteen years old. Now a half century later, I can revisit her cards and notes, letting her penmanship rekindle other joyous memories: when I put Creepy Crawlers in her bed and she screamed in mock horror to my delight; the many Saturday nights that we'd watch *The Mary Tyler Moore Show* together, eating dinner side-by-side from our TV trays; taking her mink coat when she'd arrive at our house, bringing it upstairs to my parents' room, and then rolling around in it, trying to absorb her scent; and even her very last days, after she'd had a series of strokes, when I'd sit by her side, holding her hand, wiping her brow, and telling her how much I loved her. It's as though Grandma's handwriting has bestowed eternal life on her—and us.

## Write On: Reclaiming Your Script

I am guessing that, like many people, you've fallen out of the habit of writing almost anything by hand. You text or email friends to make plans, to catch up, even to send birthday greetings. Can you remember when you last wrote out a card or letter in your best penmanship? I didn't think so.

I'm going to offer you two different challenges here. Choose the one that appeals to you or do both!

### THE GREETING CARD CHALLENGE

Check to see which of your friends or family members has a birthday or other special date coming up. Two weeks or so in advance of that date, buy a card. Don't just sign it, but instead handwrite a note within the card. Take some time to reflect on what you have to say. If you're not sure what to say, you can always write about what's going on in your life and ask about what's going on with them. Then mail the card to them. After you're fairly certain they've received it, follow up with a text, email, or even a phone call, and ask how it made them feel to get a written note—that is, if they haven't contacted you already to thank you!

## THE MYSTERY WRITER CHALLENGE

Send an actual letter to a friend—yes, via snail mail, to their physical home address—but don't sign it or include a return address. Explain that you are trying to reconnect on a deeper level, and you want to find out if they recognize you by your handwriting. Try not to reveal your identity, but feel free to drop some hints about how you're connected, like attending the same high school or volunteering at a specific nonprofit. Ask them to text or email you if they think they can figure out who you are. The worst that can happen is they reconnect with other friends before figuring out it was you. (If you think your recipient might find this anxiety-inducing—"What if I guess incorrectly?"—send your message without asking for anything in return. The worst that can happen is that they know someone is thinking about them.)

## EXTRA CREDIT

Think about how it made you feel to hold pen in hand and form your words more thoughtfully than you would at a keyboard or with your fingers. As the final challenge, write a note to yourself about how this experiment went, mail it to yourself, and see what you experience when it arrives and you open it.

# THE JOY OF PERSPECTIVE

Several years ago, I found myself lost near Big Sur, California. It was night, and fog had encircled me, erasing the full moon that would have helped me find the path back to my friend's house. I stopped and waited, anxiety building, when suddenly I took several steps toward a breach in the fog. The moon, uncovered again, revealed the way forward. A few tiny steps—with a bit of a turn—and my entire perspective had changed.

I understood the metaphor: change your perspective to change your life. I've heard it many times over many decades. For the longest time I thought it was New Age pablum. I've read various articles about this very subject, from "11 Ways to Change Your Perspective and Be More Positive ASAP" to "5 Ways to Change Your Perspective and Be Happier." I'm sorry, is it five or eleven? And is it at all realistic?

This cynical interior monologue came back to me several years ago as I attended an evening of dance, song, and spoken word created by patients in Memorial Sloan Kettering Cancer Center's Visible Ink program, a free writing initiative for patients undergoing treatment. Since 2008, more than three thousand individuals and three hundred mentors (including myself) have participated in this innovative program. For fifteen springs, Visible Ink's artistic director, Greg Kachejian, has stitched together a one-night-only performance, delivered by Broadway actors who volunteer their time and artistry.

The last year before the pandemic turned the in-person show into a Zoom event. I sat in the auditorium as various pieces were performed. When an actor began a dramatic reading of a poem, "All I Want," penned by Sarah Porwoll, I bolted upright in my seat. As I learned later, Sarah, an advertising executive, had recently completed treatment for breast cancer. "I was thirty-two years old and the diagnosis came as quite a shock. Cancer is never anything anybody expects, but especially in my early thirties, I really didn't expect it." Only six days earlier, her boyfriend, Matt, had proposed to her. "It was a very intense time, going from sharing the news of being engaged with all my friends and family to then letting everybody know I was about to go through surgery and everything that was about to happen." Listening to Sarah, I wondered how she—but really, anyone—could hold such different emotions at the same time, referring to the sorrow of her diagnosis and the joy of her engagement.

I decided to call an expert, Matthew Kuan Johnson, a philosopher who wrote the lead article for a special issue on joy in *The*

*Journal of Positive Psychology*. Johnson had also been thinking about this very question, explaining to me succinctly, "Because it's not a choice." When I asked him to elaborate, I heard the passion in his words. "The reason why we find so much joy amidst just absolutely devastating and unspeakable suffering is because you need to find joy in those contexts. Otherwise, life is literally unbearable. Joy is this incredible act of survival, but also of resistance, of asserting that I am going to actually make a demand of life, of specifically what it refuses to give me." He helped to buttress my now expanding view of joy, as I continued to understand that my almost simple understanding of joy—ecstasy! delight!—needed an upgrade.

Robert Emmons, a scholar of gratitude and joy, has also wrestled with this question, although he's come to a somewhat different understanding. In an interview broadcast online, Emmons explains that in addition to experiencing joy as an emotion, "one can also have an attitude of joyfulness, which says that despite what's happening in my life, I'm going to choose to be joyful." In that interview, he refers to the apostle Paul, who incorporates the word "joy" sixteen times in his letter to the Philippians, expressing optimism in the face of death. "Where is he when he's writing that letter?" asks Emmons. "He's in prison. He's awaiting a trial that could result in his death, and he is joyful nevertheless. It's almost a spirit of defiant joyfulness, which is really a chosen attitude because you're not going to feel joy in the situation. But you can choose to adopt joy as an attitude to help you really transcend that circumstance."

The six months following Sarah's diagnosis tested her. She had a lumpectomy and sixteen rounds of chemo followed by weeks of radiation. With her sweet laugh, she added, "I was also planning the wedding, which was a welcome distraction. My fiancé and I used my chemo sessions to stuff and stamp save-the-date invitations and plan our honeymoon to Spain. I thankfully was connected to a kind and talented hair and makeup stylist who had experience with wigs. She did an incredible job transforming my everyday wig into the perfect low-bun hairstyle I'd always hoped to have for my wedding day."

Sarah told me that during the months of treatment and wedding planning she had to stay laser-focused "on just getting through everything, which didn't leave a lot of time to process." Only later did she start to jot down random feelings and thoughts about her illness, hoping that writing might help her better understand all she'd been through. "That's when I wrote my first poem," she explained.

A year later she reached out to the Visible Ink program, and with the guidance of a writing mentor, began to write poems in earnest. In the winter of 2019, Sarah learned that her poem "All I Want" had been chosen to be performed that coming spring.

On the darkened stage, a professional actor read Sarah's poem as the words—in white letters—scrolled by on a black scrim.

I'm bored by the repetition of day-to-day life
So I rarely feel like
Each day is a gift
Now
I know
I can't explain how it feels to believe that
To be normal
Makes me feel like all I want is
The unexpected
Then my world turned upside down

After a short pause, the actor began again, this time starting with the last line of the poem, reading in reverse order.

Then my world turned upside down
The unexpected
Makes me feel like all I want is
To be normal
I can't explain how it feels to believe that
I know
Now
Each day is a gift
So I rarely feel like
I'm bored by the repetition of day-to-day life

The audience gasped as the reading ended; then we applauded loudly. The change in perspective had completely altered the poem's meaning.

"Watching my poem being performed onstage was honestly thrilling," Sarah recounted. "I was so nervous people might not 'get it.' Hearing the crowd respond as they did before the clapping began let me know they did indeed understand what I wanted them to take away. Looking back now, I remember grinning ear to ear, laughing, full of joy and relief, but my husband, sister, and friend who had come to support me were all misty-eyed and relatively quiet. They knew what I had gone through—what they had all helped me get through—to get to this point, and I think their joy just came through in a different way." Sarah's point struck me, as this was when I began to understand how the language of joy may vary—in this instance, from laughter to crying.

When I asked Sarah what the poem meant to her, she explained, "It's about the shift in perspective I've had, now that I've had even more time between everything that happened and where I am today. I would catch myself feeling like, 'Oh, I'm just riding the subway. I'm going to work. I'm coming home, I'm doing chores.' That's what I craved the most when I was going through treatment—to think about the normal things I would think about in a day, to not have the struggles that came along with going through treatment. I find myself needing to remind myself of the joy that can come in the everyday things."

These days, so many years later, Sarah says, "I often recite my poem, forward and backward, if I'm frustrated about a situation or feeling down. It reminds me to be grateful for normalcy in a way

I hadn't before. And I think we all, especially after living through the Covid-19 pandemic, have a new appreciation for finding joy in 'normalcy.'"

In the fall of 2020, Sarah lost her job. But she said that instead of "dwelling on my circumstance, I chose to see the joy of taking much-needed time away from the stress of work and constant Zoom meetings." The Porwolls had recently bought a house in the Catskills, so they focused on enjoying nature and settling into a slower routine. They also began the IVF process. "Today I feel blessed to be a mom to an adorable, clever, and healthy baby boy, Julian," she was happy to tell me.

"Finding joy in the everyday is easy with Julian. His contagious giggles, endless curiosity, and the way his face lights up when he learns something new—blowing a kiss, where his nose is, standing on his own—make each 'normal' moment something to be cherished. Even on the hard days, just seeing his sweet face reminds me how lucky I am to be living this life."

As for me, how often have I felt trapped by where I am or what I'm seeing, even though there aren't any walls confining me? With time I've come to see that those blinders are within me—not on the outside—and that I actually have the wherewithal to take a step in a different direction, to seek to see in a new light, to intentionally shift my perspective, allowing me to experience joy where I hadn't before. Curiously, as I am finishing up this chapter, I'm looking out over a forest of muted brown and gray trees, made barren and bleak by the winter. Then my mind wanders a bit, and I can see the quiet beauty of this monochromatic scene. My focus intensifies, and I realize the spring buds are also present, nascent, waiting to burst forth as gorgeous foliage, which . . . will suffocate me in pollen in no time. Wait, wait, wrong perspective. What I meant to say . . . which symbolizes the full-throated renewal that comes with the spring. I will choose joy.

## How Do You Define What a Day Is Worth to You?

Brad Lea is an entrepreneur, motivational speaker, and podcaster. His books and podcast episodes are more likely to focus on building wealth than anything else. But when he made a guest appearance on the *Millionaire Mindsets* podcast, he surprised his hosts by challenging them with what appeared to be a simple question, which I'm paraphrasing: Would you be happy if I gave you $10 million right now? Of course! they answered. Then came the kicker. Would they still take the money if it meant they would not wake up tomorrow?

It's a startling question indeed. I know I wouldn't take that trade. In fact, I think few people would. What's the point of all that money if you are not alive to enjoy it?

Alas, I'm not going to offer you $10 million—not even $1 million—but tomorrow, and the next day, I challenge you to wake up as if your day were worth more than $10 million and think about what you're going to do with that precious day. When I tried this on myself, I gave my dog an extra-long walk, called an old friend out of the blue, invited some neighbors over for no special reason, and reread some of Mary Oliver's poems. What was all that worth to me? As the vintage Mastercard commercials repeated endlessly, "Priceless."

What can you do tomorrow to change your perspective on how you live? Write it down. What happened? How did you feel?

# THE JOY OF THE CANCER WARD

I can't be late tonight," I murmured to myself as I dashed out of the Rockefeller Center skyscraper where I worked, running smack-dab into an army of holiday tourists, all visiting the famous Christmas tree. Weaving through the crowd, probably appearing a bit tipsy to those tourists, I knew I had to be nimble if I wanted to stay on schedule. "Hurry up!" I whispered under my breath. "I have an appointment to keep."

Arriving at the hospital, I was surprised—as I was every week—to see my reflection in the smoky-dark glass sliding doors and then see, etched in the glass, the name of the building: Memorial Sloan Kettering Cancer Center.

Throttling my fear, I took a deliberate step through the doors, then rode the escalator up one level to the hospital lobby. This year it was decked out in a sea of crimson and white poinsettias for the holidays. Alas, it was impossible to escape the Christmas Muzak wafting through the cavernous space.

My history with Memorial Sloan Kettering goes back to 1984, to the warm June evening when the hospital admitted me for the first time. I was twenty-six years old and had only days before been diagnosed with metastatic testicular cancer. I'd already complained to the night nurse about the polyester-blend sheets and the cardboard-like pillows. Only when I looked back did I understand, that was my fear speaking in tongues. Later that evening, a tall man wearing a pale blue coat visited me. He identified himself only as Alan. I don't recall much else of what he told me, except a few words about having been a "patient here once" and something about having been "your age at the time." After about ten minutes I looked up at him. "Oh, so you're a cancer survivor. Cool." He nodded yes, showed me the long scar on his belly, and then left me a precious gift: hope.

Thirteen years later, on that cold December evening in 1997, I was back at Memorial Sloan Kettering. Only this time, I wasn't the guy in the bed facing his mortality. This time I was the fellow in the blue hospital coat, as I'd joined the hospital's Patient-to-Patient Peer Support Group, which paired breast cancer survivors with breast cancer patients, prostate with prostate, and (in my case) testicular cancer survivors with newly diagnosed testicular cancer patients. Our goal was simple: to give newly diagnosed patients the opportunity to connect with someone who had walked their walk, to let them know they were not alone.

Each week, I'd check in at the volunteer office on the first floor, don that blue coat, say hello to a few other volunteers, and walk over to the M elevator, traveling to the eighth floor, then the home of the urology ward. I'd pick up my assignment—first name and room number—from the head social worker and night nurses. No matter the season, the mood of the floor was unfailingly calm and bright. Nurses, aides, and the occasional doctor passed from room to room bringing succor and a smile to their patients. There looked to be a choreography to the movement, graceful and considered. (When something did go awry, a team would rush into the patient's room, closing the door to the rest of us.) Each week, from the first, I experienced a rare, inexplicable feeling of focus and tranquility while on the floor.

I didn't understand this as joy. I'd long held on to the notion that there's an intensity to joy, that it's linked to what's known as the dopaminergic system, which fuels our drives and urges. But researchers now understand that "serene joy" is a counterpart to "excited joy"; the quieter and calmer sibling, it results in feelings of harmony and unity. Specifically, it aims at restoring the body to equilibrium, which is precisely how I'd describe what I experienced each week at the hospital.

On this particular December evening, I visited a fellow I'll call Peter. In addition to having "my" cancer, Peter was in 821, my old room. Curled up in bed, with just wisps of hair on his head and a baby-soft face, Peter looked more like a fourteen-year-old boy than the forty-year-old dad he was. I greeted him tentatively.

"My name is Steven," I began. "I'm a hospital volunteer . . . in the Patient-to-Patient program."

I kept it short. We're instructed not to say the word "cancer," because we don't know what patients actually understand about their disease.

Peter beckoned me to sit with a wave of his arm (the one not attached to an IV) and continued to watch television. I approached and looked at the screen, and then looked at him. Again, I looked at the screen and a moment later at him. I guess he's in no rush, I thought to myself. And, you know what? Neither was I. We sat together quietly, he in his bed and me in an uncomfortable recliner, both looking at the TV screen.

Even though I didn't mention the word "cancer," Peter knew what was wrong with him. Finally, he started talking. He told me about his orchiectomy (the surgical procedure to remove a cancerous testicle), and I told him about mine. He recounted his chemo experience (particularly with the harsh platinum drugs), and I told him about mine. I asked him if he wanted to see my scar, as Alan had once done for me. He shook his head no.

No matter, I could tell he was really paying attention, his eyes focused on my head—especially my hair. Yes, I had hair again. Suddenly, it was as if all the pieces had come into focus, and Peter asked, incredulously: "You're a cancer survivor?"

"Yes, I am," I said to him, explaining I'd been in that same room some thirteen years before.

And just like that I could see that I'd transformed into a gift called hope. It was actually a regift—thank you, Alan—but this regifting carried no stigma. The deeper truth is that every patient

I talked to or sat with during the years I volunteered at Memorial Sloan Kettering also gave me a gift.

Was my willingness to volunteer related to my earlier experience in the hospital? Did my brother and sister also become volunteers because they saw how well I'd been tended to by a small army of people giving their time freely to others? It's possible, said Jamil Zaki, an associate professor of psychology at Stanford University who has spent years studying how kindness can be transmitted. "We find that people imitate not only the particulars of positive actions, but also the spirit underlying them," according to his 2016 article in *Scientific American*. "This implies that kindness itself is contagious, and that it can cascade across people, taking on new forms along the way." For instance, he found that people made larger charitable gifts when they believed others were generous than when they thought people around them were stingy. Even more interesting, Zaki learned that when people cannot afford to donate money, "an individual's kindness can nonetheless trigger people to spread positivity in other ways."

That is what's known as the kindness contagion, Zaki explained to me on the phone. "When we see other people around us acting in generous or kind or empathic ways, we will be more inclined to act that way ourselves," he continued.

As I've mentioned, I'm not exactly a silver-linings kind of guy, but wow, I'm glad that I've been able to play a small role in creating some kind of good from some kind of bad. Jonas Nguh, a registered nurse and professor of nursing at Walden University, writes wisely online, "Volunteering gives you a lot in return. It is all about the joy of making a difference . . . while receiving immense value . . . from the experience of volunteering, meeting people and learning something new."

---

At another time, under different circumstances, Martin Luther King Jr., the civil rights leader, spoke about the joy of giving: "Life's most persistent and urgent question is, 'What are you doing for others?'" A more contemporary voice, Deepak Chopra writes in *The Seven Spiritual Laws of Success* that practicing the joy of giving is actually quite simple. "If you want joy, give joy to others; if you want love, learn to give love; if you want attention and appreciation, learn to give attention and appreciation. . . . If you want to be blessed with all the good things in life, learn to silently bless everyone with all the good things in life." Simple, perhaps. Rewarding, most certainly.

I don't want to sound like one of those As Seen On TV ads, always promising, "But wait, there's more!" But wait, there *is* more we do receive by giving, especially in terms of documented health benefits. When we help others, our brains secrete "feel good" chemicals such as serotonin (helping to regulate mood), dopamine (giving a sense of pleasure), and oxytocin (creating a sense of connection with others). "When we do things for other people, it makes us feel much more engaged and joyful," Cleveland Clinic psychologist Susan Albers writes, adding, "That's good for our health and our happiness." To boot, new research is deepening our understanding of the positive correlation between volunteering and a feeling of well-being or joy, according to a research paper published in the *Journal of Happiness Studies.* That study found that those who volunteered more often were more satisfied with their lives when compared with those who didn't. What's more, the frequency of volunteering was correlated with greater satisfaction. Those who reported volunteering at least once a month experienced better mental health benefits. In other words, the more you volunteer (both in frequency and duration), the more joyful you will become.

The week after meeting Peter I returned for another volunteer shift at the hospital. I changed into my pale blue coat, then set off to a different floor to visit a woman I'll call Maryann, in her forties. She'd been diagnosed with advanced cancer of the appendix. (We became a match because the hospital had no surviving appendix cancer patients in our program to pair with her. I was the make-do.)

Maryann described to me how her most recent surgery had not held. I wasn't sure what she meant by that, but I only had to wait a moment. "On my first day home, fecal matter had begun to leak from my navel. . . ." Then, she asked me point-blank, "Were you ever afraid during your treatment?" I answered yes, feeling as though I'd entered a zone of safety with her where we could be open, honest, and vulnerable. I described to Maryann the horrible night toward the end of my months of chemo when I'd become undone by a torrent of puke and tears. "I had canker sores in my mouth," I said. "I'd lost more than twenty pounds and had to sleep with a pillow between my bony knees. And my thick brown hair had long ago fallen out, first in wisps, then in clumps," I prattled on. "Yes, I was afraid."

Curiously enough, only as I finished my story did I realize how much resilience I'd developed since that time. I felt a sudden joy in being able to remember that summer and share it with Maryann. To that point, Ingrid Fetell Lee, author of *Joyful,* writes, "Celebrating small joys with others deepens our bonds and increases our sense of trust that we'll be there for each other when things go wrong."

When it was time for me to leave, Maryann thanked me for visiting, and I thanked her for showing me her courage and reminding me of mine.

After I said good night to Maryann, which I did with a hug, I took the elevator down to the main floor and shed my blue coat, then phoned in my report to the social worker on call.

A century before, the British novelist E. M. Forster had written, "Only connect," speaking to the importance of our relationships to help defeat "the isolation" that keeps us apart. Ironically, I felt more connection—to strangers!—during my Tuesdays at Memorial Sloan Kettering than I did during the rest of the week with friends, family, and colleagues. I experienced a lightness, a sense of liberation.

Moments after making my call, I approached the sliding glass doors and walked out onto the wide expanse of York Avenue. I thought to myself, "All is calm. All is bright."

## Walter and Maria

I've found it beyond satisfying to volunteer with the Visible Ink writing program, helping patients and their caregivers use their words to tell their stories. If anything, I'd say it's transformed me.

In the fall of 2019, when I was still a relatively new writing mentor, the program director paired me with Walter Schubert, then sixty-one. A gay man (like me), he'd survived an advanced cancer (like me) and then found himself taking care of his younger sister with an incurable cancer (like me). I worked with him on his essay for months; at the same time, his sister Maria continued to fail. She died before Walter finished "Visitors," which was published the following spring in the program's annual collection. I loved the wisdom and grace of this passage, which comes from his story.

> Life surprises us this way, constantly opening us up to something new. Everything that comes is just a visitor—the house sparrow, the leaves waving, the scents surrounding us, and our feelings too. They are all just visitors. They are all here now and then—poof!—gone in an instant. . . . I didn't see life this way until my cancer arrived, and after a while . . . I came to see it, too, as just a visitor.

After we had finished our work together, Walter wrote to thank me, which proved to be a gift beyond measure. How unexpected. How gratifying.

To be frank, working with Walter had not been easy for me, given his disease and his sister's illness, an experience so close to mine and Julie's. At the end of many of our conversations, I felt the wound within me, bloodied and raw. I experienced times when I wanted to bail, but how could I, when Maria was dying, while Walter was doing his best?

In the several years since Walter wrote his essay, I've returned to it for inspiration, to remember the abiding love he shared with his sister and the immense pain of her death, and Walter's resilience throughout. What a gift he gave me. Or as Gandhi once said, "The best way to find yourself is to lose yourself in the service of others."

# THE JOY OF PLAY

During the fall of 2022, my sister was hospitalized every week as she began a new clinical trial for the cancer that continued to outsmart conventional therapies. The research chief told us up front, "It's better to be safe than sorry."

Away from the hospital, I found myself learning to play Qwirkle, a tile-based game, which one friend describes as "Scrabble without the letters and ten times more fun to play." It also requires a decent amount of strategy, which can take time to pick up, although the instruction manual boasts the game is for anyone six or over. And a lot of luck, but no one ever tells you that. I struggled for the first few rounds as my friend Hunter Hallmark kept making one Qwirkle after another. (You score a Qwirkle when you complete a line of all six colors or shapes.) Then, ginned up by a run of good fortune (because it certainly couldn't be skill), I won my first game. "Qwirkle!" I shouted each time I made one. Hip, hip, hurrah for me! I was the epitome of graciousness in winning. Not!

One of our postgame text threads displayed the high stakes—and fun—in a game that included Hunter's mother, Jo Ann, who is also my friend.

> JO ANN: Hunter broke 200 in the second game!
>
> STEVEN: I'm suspicious.
>
> HUNTER: I was the only one keeping score.
>
> STEVEN: Exactly my concern. How can you do that to your mom?
>
> HUNTER: Very few morals during game play.
>
> JO ANN: Nope, it was fair and square! I actually cheated a couple of times.
>
> STEVEN: Remember, it's not whether you win or lose, it's how you play the game.
>
> HUNTER: I'm just so glad I could bring Qwirkle into your lives. Thank you, Qwirkle, for bringing us all a little closer.

There's nothing like a competitive game to bring out the champ—and the cheater—in each of us. Mostly, though, it's about the enjoyment—joy!—of being together in real life, reminding me of the board and card games I'd played as a kid with my own family—everything from hearts, blackjack, and poker, to Scrabble, Risk, and Monopoly, which I excelled at (perhaps because I was always the banker!). It also brought back happy memories of being that kid who knew the joy of play.

Where had he gone?

Smiley Poswolsky, the author of *Friendship in the Age of Loneliness* and a motivational speaker on the topic of workplace culture, is something of an expert on the joys of game playing: "We're constantly performing for other people, or we're constantly asked to play by somebody else's rules. What happens when you just give people the job of play? 'You get to go play now. You get to do whatever you want. You get to be whoever you want.' It's pretty profound." Sadly, it's all too often passé.

Smiley learned a lot about the joy of play during his long tenure as a counselor at Camp Grounded, a summer retreat for adults. For more than five years,* Camp Grounded, where "grown-ups go . . . to get away . . . and be kids again," hosted between 250 and 300 campers each summer. Upon arrival, you'd check your devices and agree not to talk about work. Campers shed their names (which is to say their identities) and took on new monikers, like Honey Bear, Twizzleman McBean, Cookie Surprise, Prow Prow, Brickey St. James, and Professor Wigglesworth. Smiley, whose real name is Adam, told me how our names carry baggage; dropping them is

*Camp Grounded hosted campers for five seasons and closed after founder Levi Felix died from a brain tumor in 2017, at age thirty-two.

a way for people to shed their usual skins, their job titles, and approach life in a different way. Another counselor, Brady Gill, explained it to me this way: "I know what Brady can and can't do, but Honey Bear [his nickname] . . . maybe he can do more. Many chose nicknames that were aspirational and served as a reminder to focus on their intention."

With a smile in his voice—yes, I could hear it—Smiley detailed the many activities at camp, which included color wars, a talent show, a dance, arts and crafts, sing-alongs, and face painting, as well as some "regular" activities like kickball, rock climbing, stargazing, and archery. "So much of the joy is in the moment," Smiley told me. "When I look back at the photos of camp, you see so much joy and face paint and the screaming and the people rooting on their teammates during color wars." He also pointed out that time for play gives us "space enough for people to have clarity of thought and clarity of purpose and self that our normal day-to-day lives don't offer that much of." We're cracked open, in a sense, able to awaken our younger selves.

Yoga teacher Coby Kozlowski agrees with this idea that play and joy are intertwined. "The joyful, playful side of the inner journey often gets overlooked. There's often guilt in joy because there's so much suffering in the world, so a lot of people are resistant to it," she said. Similarly, Erin Maile O'Keefe, who co-teaches a CircusYoga workshop at Kripalu, a retreat center in western Massachusetts, sees play as a process of refinding the childlike wonder we shed as we get older, of rediscovering our curiosity about the world surrounding us and within us. "Play," she said, "is about taking risks—we discover something new about ourselves."

Until the pandemic, I last played tennis in the summer of 1974, which is when Richard Nixon resigned the presidency. I was seventeen. That August I'd won the singles tournament for juniors in our village. As recognition, I was awarded a small, faux gold trophy of a tennis player in mid-serve. At best I was an okay player, but I played with a joie de vivre. I took this statuette to college with me, then grad school, keeping it front and center wherever I lived. While its presence remained constant, its meaning morphed over time, proving to be less about winning and more about the enjoyment I'd taken on the court with others. Win or lose, tennis had been fun.

I stopped playing soon after that victory. It wasn't a conscious decision, but looking back I didn't think I had time for that kind of fun. Adulting would demand I spend my time on more productive and important pursuits. Fast-forward almost fifty years: As pandemic restrictions were lifted in 2021, our town began to offer tennis clinics anew. On a whim I signed up. Tennis had brought me joy in the past; maybe it would again?

After the first session on a not-too-warm summer evening, I told a friend, "I loved playing tonight, even though I am the worst player on the court." Two weeks later, I emailed a friend to say I was loving the game, especially meeting new people outside of my usual circle and playing outdoors. "Oh, and I'm getting better. I am now the second-worst player."

Scott Davis, a movement therapist and yoga teacher, refers to this notion as "embracing the suck." I laughed when he used that phrase, a common military expression, which he clarified to mean accepting the unpleasant, even the failures, in pursuit of eventual success. "I think it's key to do things you're not good at," he told me over a Zoom call. "Get over the ego side of having to be good, and then you can just feel the joy of failing." Or, in my case, the joy of being second-worst.

While on the court, I also feel very much connected to my younger self, a Steven who lived in the moment, accepted himself (for the most part), did not worry about perfectionism, and could try new things simply because he enjoyed them.

I'm now in my second year back playing tennis, where I'm learning to listen to my body and trust in its wisdom. In my most recent tennis update on Facebook, I posted: "I continue to have so much fun on the court, with new friends and coaches. Now I'm only the fourth-worst player!" I've clearly embraced my suck.

We also now know that tennis, like most cardio exercises, has other benefits; it reduces inflammation in the brain, which can eventually lead to depression, anxiety, and loneliness. "Regular exercise also remodels the physical structure of your brain to make you more receptive to joy and social connection," wrote Kelly McGonigal in *The Joy of Movement.*

If I'm going to be completely honest, I've also realized one other, more important benefit of my time on the court. The focus that tennis demands prevents me from any kind of mind wandering, especially to real-world problems like my sister's illness. For one hour I can forget everything, except keeping my eye on the ball and paying attention to my form.

Whether it's Qwirkle or tennis, playing for fun—as opposed to playing to win—goes against my competitive nature, my understanding of what it means to be an adult. Then again, adulting—which means doing things that are boring, tiresome, and joyless—may not be such a great thing after all. As the popular saying goes, "We don't stop playing because we grow old; we grow old because we stop playing."

## How to Experience the Joy of Play

Researchers have documented play behavior in most animal species, especially in infants and juveniles, but they disagree on why exactly we play. Play may have an evolutionary purpose in helping youngsters learn the rules of their social organization or develop cognitive skills that will help them in the wild. Maybe it's just fun!

Scott Davis is a big fan of play, and he's definitely in the camp of those who find it to be an important and complex element of learning and development. He doesn't underestimate the role of fun, though, and he would love for more of us to set aside our idea of "adulting" long enough to remember the joy of play.

"By the time we're adults, most of us have unlearned how to play," he said. Conditioned to compete instead of play, to accomplish instead of enjoy, we lose our natural state of playfulness—and with it, we lose the joy. Davis has a road map for reigniting that innate sense of play and finding that joy, no matter how long it's been since you felt it.

**First and foremost, forget about the concept of winning.** Choose a game, activity, or sport that you want to *play*. As you learn, you are going to make mistakes, fail, and lose (a lot). Accept that you are not in it to win it, but to play it, and embrace your failures as learning opportunities.

**Choose an activity that you are truly curious about.** Davis advises us to get into the "beginner's mind," or shoshin, as it is known in Zen Buddhism. Even if it's something you've done before, get into the beginner's mind and approach the activity from a new perspective, with no preconceptions about where your play will take you.

**Set goals and boundaries that are not about winning.** Don't play until you achieve mastery over a new skill, but instead for a set amount of time, or until you're tired. Accentuate the play, not the achievement.

**Keep it playful.** Stay focused on your interest in the play, your pleasure in it, and your curiosity about it. If you're worried about "getting it right" or winning, you're losing your sense of play!

Davis said he believes that play is useful for improving communication, sparking creativity, and strengthening cooperation, but the primary goal for engaging in it should be fun, not self-improvement. Consider all the benefits to mind and body to be icing on the cake—the cake itself is the simple joy of play.

# THE JOY OF DOING NOTHING

My grandmother always had an aphorism on the tip of her tongue. The mantra she most often repeated was this: "Busy people are happy people." I thought of this aphorism often during the early days of the pandemic. With the increased isolation from stay-at-home orders—with restaurants, theaters, and many businesses closed—I felt like I was being forced to do nothing, and my malaise deepened daily.

But, in fact, there's no data to show that hyper-busy people are more joyful than those who are less caught up in the hamster wheel of doing. I think we all know people who declare "I'm so busy" as a way to decline a professional or personal invitation, whether to break bread, go for a walk, take a meeting, or even speak on the phone. Yes, time is one of our most precious commodities because we can't make more of it. When we use those three little words what we're often really saying is "You're not important enough for me to spend time with." That hurts, builds walls, and can even lead to the kind of toxic divisiveness we are witnessing more and more.

Or, staying busy simply distracts us from feeling bad. "I don't have time to feel" can also be heard as "I can't connect with what you're going through." That has sometimes been my own experience in avoiding sorrow, loss, or grief. Oliver Burkeman, the author of *Four Thousand Weeks*, quotes a Dutch work expert who argues how "[busyness] can be a very protective [defense] mechanism for warding off disturbing thoughts and feelings."

In fact, the opposite may be true, meaning that overly busy people are neither happy nor joyful (sorry, Grandma). A pre-pandemic report from the Pew Research Center found that 60 percent of adults in the United States said they felt too busy to enjoy life, with most of us trying to do at least two things at once. Burkeman adds his two cents here, writing that "too much busyness is counterproductive," meaning we too often confuse effort with effectiveness.

Midway through the pandemic, I listened to meditation teacher Jeff Warren talk about his Do Nothing Project, which he humorously described as an "experiment in . . . doing not much together." He led the live stream on YouTube from his living room in Toronto, surrounded by big cushy pillows and a philodendron that appeared to be growing out of his head. Each week Warren reminded us that "we can use the time to doodle, stare vacantly into space, or meditate, which is again pretty much about doing nothing." He promised, "It's a training in equanimity." Really? Would doing nothing help me find inner calm? Would doing nothing help me find joy? I thought doing nothing would make me nuts, actually. But I was mistaken. As I realized, there are times when there's much to be learned or unpacked in letting our minds wander freely. I've now been attending the live stream for a couple of years, one of a few hundred people who join in real time from all over the world.

The practice of "doing nothing" has been popularized by several recent books, one of which is the 2020 book *Niksen* by Olga Mecking. According to Mecking, the best way to define *niksen*, a Dutch word, is "doing nothing on purpose, without a purpose," which differentiates it from other self-care activities like yoga, breadmaking, joining a book club, or volunteering at a local nonprofit, all of which have an ostensible goal. She argues that doing nothing is an alternative to the pressure many of us feel to have our days scheduled for maximum productivity. (Although Mecking acknowledged that some of us will find it necessary to schedule our "do nothing" time, which is called *niks* in Dutch.)

In any case, I quickly picked up on the distinction between choosing to do nothing (like joining Jeff's group) and being forced to do nothing (thank you, Covid).

I thought about some young people I know—including myself as a kid—who are given the freedom to daydream, to get lost in their thoughts. For instance, as an eight-year-old, I'd go up to my bedroom, lie down on the bed, and imagine myself traveling the world on a magic carpet. A truly fantastic voyage. But then as school became more rigorous—with more homework, after-school activities, and chores—I found myself daydreaming less and less. Who had the time to do nothing? Not me then. Not me now. What I didn't realize is that when I stopped letting my mind wander, my world got smaller.

What happens when you do nothing? A lot, as it turns out, although I've found you have to do a little work to get there. When I've done meditation previously, I usually bounced back and forth between being fidgety, distracted, bored, or irritated. Jeff's group is a different experience, in part because he advises us to keep expectations low, often reminding us that we can exit anytime by clicking the "leave" button. Yes, there's an escape hatch!

Jeff doesn't tout greater focus, lower blood pressure, or reduced stress, some of the known benefits of meditation. If anything, he hopes people will be able to "just to sit there and . . . be a human being without compulsively needing to upgrade your situation." Or, put another way, "to find genuine rest in the middle of the busyness."

~

David Vago, a core faculty member at the Vanderbilt Brain Institute, studies neuropsychology and is quite familiar with both Jeff's work and the larger practice of mindful meditation. Neuroscientists, Vago says, refer to the passive daydreamy state of "doing nothing" as the default resting state for the mind. Our brains require this downtime not only to recharge, but to process all the data we're deluged with, to consolidate memory, and to reinforce learning. Anything that gets in the way of all that can be detrimental to health. It's also been called "mind wandering," a phrase that takes me back to that childhood magic carpet. When we deliberately allow our minds to wander, Vago told me, they can move toward content that is helpful and adaptive—or self-reflective and maladaptive. Mind wandering, at its best, can be constructive for creativity or focused planning. "I'd like more of that," I said to myself.

By the end of my second Do Nothing Project session, my mind had begun to quiet. Less fidgety, for sure. I noticed that breathing deeply—in through my nose, out through my mouth—calmed me. I could tell that my heart rate had fallen (which I later corroborated with an at-home monitor). I stopped thinking about my to-do list (even what to make for dinner afterward), my sister's illness, the topsy-turvy state of the world, and the deadlines I had coming up. And I enjoyed this online community, where everyone signs in, greeting each other with high fives and enthusiastic exclamations, doing nothing together.

In the weeks and months that followed, I unearthed a new calmness, or at least the beginnings of equanimity. I came to fully realize that "doing nothing" is not actually doing nothing; it's really about doing nothing *useful*, which helps to keep me rooted in the present, and prevents me from skipping ahead to the future (where worry stalks at every corner). Ironically, that sense of peace and quiet also allows me to recharge, to see things differently, and to improve my ability to solve problems. That's not nothing; that's *something!*

Moshe Bar, a professor of neuroscience at Bar-Ilan University in Tel Aviv and the author of *Mindwandering*, told me in an interview that doing nothing is key to creativity and problem solving. "This is how good ideas are born," he said, explaining that the less stressed we are, the further our minds can roam. Mind wandering also helps us to experience joy, which Bar notes can mean different things. "But they all involve positive mood." When we're preoccupied with worries and ruminations, we can let our minds wander only narrowly. When we let our minds travel more broadly, which is to say freely and creatively, that's when we're most likely to experience a positive mood change.

We often feel guilty and judge ourselves harshly when we're not "productive" with our time. Bar urges us against feeling that way. "Not feeling guilty in general will magnify our joy in life, and when you add to this the great mood that comes with free and unrestricted wandering, as well as the creative ideas that result from it, you've got yourself a recipe for ample joy."

I've learned that I can "do nothing" almost anywhere. For me, it helps to have a designated time (like the Do Nothing Project's weekly meeting), or you can put a hold on your calendar (say fifteen or thirty minutes a day). I'm finding that I can "do nothing" on walks, while swimming, even while washing the dishes or folding the laundry. It's a mindset more than anything else. As the tattoo on Jeff's right forearm reads, "let go." Relaxation jump-starts rejuvenation.

## How to Do Nothing

I've been "doing nothing" with Jeff Warren on Sunday nights for two years now. It's only thirty-five minutes, but it's such an important part of my week. (Tune in to Jeff's YouTube channel on Sunday nights to do nothing in real time, or come back anytime to view the recorded stream.) Jeff kindly agreed to create a special Do Nothing for us.

> Eyes open or closed, whatever's comfortable. Maybe start with a few slow breaths. Just being a body here, breathing.
>
> *Pause*
>
> Imagine you have come home after a long day's work, and for whatever reason, you have a window of ten minutes where you don't need to be anywhere, and nobody is expecting you.
>
> You can just sit on your front stoop—or porch, or fire escape—and just exist.
>
> Idly listening to the sound of traffic, or crickets, or the hum of a vent. And there is nowhere you need to be, and nowhere else you *want* to be.

That's the invitation. Can you just sit and exist and appreciate this opportunity to take a break?

*Pause*

Good. Just sitting and existing. Unhurried.

You might find yourself paying attention to the breath, or sounds. Or not paying attention to anything.

You might notice the mind still galloping along, with its various worries and plans.

That's fine. No need to stop any of that. Just bring your attention back to being a body. Let any thinking unspool all on its own.

*Pause*

Just sit there being a body, breathing. Sounds are happening. Sights might be happening. Thoughts and feelings, just happening. And you're sitting in the middle of all of it. Letting go of any agenda.

Can you let it be a relief?

Can you enjoy this delicious . . . defiance?

Keep doing nothing.

*Pause*

Sitting here existing. In subtle ways, and sometimes not subtle ways, the mind starts problem-solving something, *anything*.

It's hilarious to notice this happen, this unconscious reflex.

And then you slump back again and do nothing.

Can you surrender so much that your whole body relaxes?

Holy laziness.

*Pause*

Doing nothing is mostly an attitude of appreciating simplicity.

It can be insightful: "Oh wow, this is hard for me." Or maybe: "I really need this."

None of this is a problem. Just coast here at the end, life streaming through.

*Pause*

And that's it. Nice job. You did nothing. It's good medicine, indeed.

# THE JOY OF IMPERFECTION

My nose—which tilts asymmetrically to the left—has long been a sore point for me. Truth be told, I've twice consulted doctors about correcting it. One of them had a plastic surgery simulator called FaceTouchUp that shows patients what they will look like with no more turkey neck, droopy eyelids, or—as in my case—a bendy nose. I'll admit, the preview was tempting.

I had good reason to be sensitive about my personal Leaning Tower of Pisa. After I wrote an essay in *The New York Times* mocking myself for getting blond highlights to cover the gray tide, taking ice baths to maintain my "youthful vigor," and—the pièce de résistance—getting an eye job to blast away my fatty eye bags, London's *Daily Mail* published a big story accusing me of being a "self-confessed vain man." The British tabloid chose a photo of my face and magnified it to the extent that readers could see inside my nostrils, with every facial imperfection enlarged. Immediately after publication, readers began leaving anonymous comments:

> "All that work and his nose is making a left-hand turn. Am I missing something?"
>
> "He forgot to do something with his nose. It's going sideways. Tie it to the opposite ear, bend it back."

The responses proved so awful that the paper quickly shut down the comments.

I've always understood that facial symmetry is often equated with classic beauty, the seemingly perfect balance of our form and features. One beauty blogger wrote, "In a Classic face, no one feature jumps out. The nose, eyes, mouth, chin, and forehead aren't remarkably large, or remarkably small, or noticeably close together, or noticeably far apart." I was no Classic, as the anonymous commenters confirmed.

Still, I know there are other ways to appreciate or define beauty.

I'm remembering my hunt for a pair of bedside table lamps at a local antique shop in San Francisco. Russell Pritchard, the proprietor, showed me a half dozen sets, but they were all too large, too gaudy, or too expensive. The pair I actually liked had but one flaw: they did not match, although their shades shared the same butterfly-on-parchment motif. "How would that look to people?" I asked Russell, worrying that friends might think I hadn't noticed their different heights or, worse, that I had lost my gay design gene.

He smiled and asked: "How many people are you expecting to view your bedside lamps?" Pushing me, he added: "Why does it matter if they aren't balanced? They're beautiful in their individuality and as a pair, perfect in their difference." Unconvinced, I skipped out.

A week later I returned to the shop and bought the fraternal twins. I'd thought about other mismatched things in my life, including the tableware I'd inherited from my mother (different pieces had come to her from various family members) to—okay, drumroll—my testicles. After I had the cancerous one removed, I chose a "men's extra-large" prosthesis, which—in all honesty—overpowered my genuine one. I loved the new one, and its origin story.

In bed that first night with my new lamps, I didn't obsess over the differences; in fact, my new perspective obscured them altogether, leaving me to delight in watching the butterflies dance before I clicked the lights off. In other words, my mismatched lamps taught me that balance is not about symmetry, but about perspective, how we see.

Shortly after the *Daily Mail* exposé, I returned from a vacation in Vieques, Puerto Rico, where my then husband and I had stayed at Hix Island House, a compound of five geometric concrete buildings that rise out of the ground amidst thirteen acres of whispering pines, palms, and bougainvillea. These structures have no windows, no air-conditioning, and no interior doors, but each loft has an outdoor shower, where only the beauty of the sky provides cover. A hilltop location allows for spectacular views of the ocean no matter where you are situated.

Over the compound's twenty-year history, cracks have appeared in these buildings, running up and down the exterior walls; wooden beams have become weathered, creating a visible affront to traditional notions of beauty and order. OCD Steven thought about calling the front desk manager to ask him to fix the cracks in our room, which would have been a lengthy and unnecessary job. It also would have meant erasing the room's imperfections, which is to say both its charm and history.

As I later learned, the "flawed" design was by design, according to John Hix, the owner and architect, who has explained the Japanese concept of wabi-sabi to many on his website. "Things Wabi are fresh and simple, a minimalism filled with quiet beauty. Wabi shuns the shiny for the weathered. It is the harmony, peace, tranquility, and modest balance that waits patiently to be discovered. Things Sabi accept the gift of time with dignity and grace; the patina of weathered concrete and wood."

During that stay, I met up with Hix and his wife, Neeva Gayle, in the study of their majestic concrete bunker with a view of the sea below. I looked at them, both then in their eighties, and understood what he meant by accepting "the gift of time with dignity and grace." A handsome couple, engaging, too, and stylishly dressed, their faces revealed the wear of their years, plus the effects of the harsh Canadian winters they'd lived through. As for me, I became an adherent of this philosophy as it applied to *architecture*. Not so fast when it came to my very own face; that would require an entirely new way to see myself in the world.

Ryotaro Matsumura, a tea ceremony master in Yokohama, Japan, and an expert on wabi-sabi, has explained that the concept is about flawed beauty and imperfect beauty, so very different than traditional Western concepts of matchy-matchy, balanced/symmetrical, or shiny beauty. He reminds us of why the shabby vest knitted by our grandma, or the broken seashell from an old friend, can become our dearest treasures. He suggests rethinking how we experience, say, those cracks in the wall, noting instead how they allow the light to shine through, leaving a unique shadow on the floor or walls within.

Leonard Koren, in his book *Wabi-Sabi for Artists, Designers, Poets & Philosophers*, sides with Matsumura, writing, "Wabi-sabi represents the exact opposite of the Western ideal of great beauty as something monumental, spectacular, and enduring." Koren argues that the allure of wabi-sabi is coming to terms with a different notion of beauty, one that is not refined, gorgeous, or perfect. It's about the acceptance of the inevitable or the "evanescence of life." He writes that "things wabi-sabi . . . record the sun, wind, rain, heat, and cold in a language of discoloration, rust, tarnish, stain, warping, shrinking, shriveling, and cracking." Nicks, bruises, scars, dents, and peeling are how it's manifested, and in an important sense those imperfections allow us to connect, to feel, maybe even to love.

I found myself very attached to what cultural psychologist Marianna Pogosyan describes as "a release from the hostage of perfection," which allows for a resilience and a commitment to find unusual beauty in the most unexpected places. "Ultimately, wabi-sabi opens space for love. Love for others, and no less for ourselves," she writes. "It is this love, according to Ryotaro Matsumura, that can lead to a deeper satisfaction with life. If we could feel it even once a day, it is this love, he notes, together with 'humility and gratitude for the sun, for water, for nature, for humans—despite all our imperfections—that can infuse our days with more meaning and fulfillment.'"

While it's taken me years, I've joyfully come to embrace my lack of symmetry and other imperfections, which is a good thing, because I have one foot that's smaller than the other, an off-center belly button thanks to my abdominal surgery, and, of course, my Leaning Tower of Pisa nose. If I were to change those features, I would be removing the very things that make me unique—that make me *me.* That's really why I plan to keep my nose the way it is—even if *Daily Mail* readers hate it. More poetically, I'd refer back to Leonard Koren's book, where he writes: "Beauty can spontaneously occur at any moment given the proper circumstances, context, or point of view. Beauty is thus an altered state of consciousness, an extraordinary moment of poetry and grace." And joy.

## Learning to Embrace Your Imperfections

It's so easy, so natural, and so unhelpful to focus on our own flaws. We make mistakes, we don't have magazine-cover bodies, we haven't had the career successes that we wanted. Other people's lives seem perfect, and ours don't measure up. Just spend five minutes on Instagram, where vacations, parties, pets, homes, and even our friends' kids *appear* perfect. Anne Lamott has given this conundrum much thought, writing, "Perfectionism is the voice of the oppressor, the enemy of the people. It will keep you cramped and insane your whole life."

What can we do so we don't hate what makes us who we are? Even better, to accept and embrace our true selves? And best of all, to learn how to love ourselves the way we are? For sure, there are a lot of New Agey philosophy types out there saying things like "You are special just as you are," and "Your flaws are your strengths in disguise." I just don't know how helpful these mantras are in changing attitudes. Here's where I chose to start:

**Make a list of people and things you believe are perfect.** Do your neighbors have a neat and well-kept house? Put them on the list. How about your boss and their well-behaved and well-dressed kids? Ditto. What about that Instagram friend who waxes to the moon about a recent vacation? List them all. Then, in a second column, write the mirror image of that supposed perfection. That tidy house—with a huge mortgage—maybe it takes hours of cleaning and neatening every week. Guess what? Maybe you don't want to do that. Your apartment is a little more cluttered, but you have more time to spend on what you want. Stop making comparisons. Understand that your imperfect home may be just right for how you want to live. Do the same for everything and everyone you think of as perfect. What are you learning? Jot it down.

**Now make a list of things you worry are imperfect about yourself.** What are the mirror images of those? Your nose is too small, your ears too large? They are the genetic remnants of your ancestors, handed down to you as reminders that they once lived. You goofed up at work? With any luck, you went through an educational experience, free of charge. Yelled at the kids instead of being a perfect TV sitcom parent? Perhaps you taught them the lesson that even parents have limits (and yourself a lesson in when to take a breath and walk away).

**Try to offset a perceived flaw with something that's positive.** For the longest time, I avoided looking at the scar that runs from my breastbone to below my navel (thank you, metastatic cancer). "A scar is a physical deformity, it's a physical difference," Jeffrey Marcus, the chief of pediatric plastic surgery at Duke University, explained to me. People too often draw conclusions or make assumptions about attractiveness, intelligence, even capability based on something they see. In my case, I hated that scar so much I'd get dressed in the dark. Over time, as the scar faded along with those frightening memories, what had once been a stark reminder of my illness became something else altogether: a testament to my survival. Reading Cormac McCarthy's *All the Pretty Horses* one afternoon, I stopped in recognition when I came upon this line: "Scars have the strange power to remind us that our past is real." Or as Duke's Jeff Marcus told me, "Some differences can be positive, too."

The fact is that life is full of trade-offs, a mix of our own choices and the hand genetics dealt us. We are all creatures of this moment in history, a marvelous soup of traits both good and bad, and we make of it what we can. I hope that once you see your lists, it will become more obvious to you that nobody is perfect. From there, it's a step or two to realize you're good enough. And maybe that's just fine—for now.

# THE JOY OF A CHRISTMAS MIRACLE

Call me Scrooge, but I once was a "bah humbug" kind of guy when it came to Christmas, especially when it came to all those "miraculous" stories of families reunited, kids' lives saved, and even suicides prevented. I'd disdained movies like *Miracle on 34th Street*, the tear-inducing Christmas story that introduced me (and the rest of the world) to cute-as-a-button Natalie Wood, and *It's a Wonderful Life*, where a despondent Jimmy Stewart is shown by an angel how awful things would have been if he'd never been born. Then, of course, there's *Home Alone*, the 1990 dark comedy about an eight-year-old boy (Macaulay Culkin) who is left behind for Christmas, only for everyone to learn a lesson or two about family.

Experience, however, can be a very persuasive teacher.

Let me jump back to the beginning of this four-legged shaggy-dog story. I was just a few months shy of my twenty-ninth birthday when I reached my two-year cancer remission anniversary—a happy milestone. No matter, I remained highly anxious and in the dumps. A few weeks later, I happened to see an ad for a litter of cocker spaniels, and spontaneously decided to pay a house call. In the backyard of a shingled cottage in Berkeley, I watched eight pups repeatedly bulldoze the ninth, the runt of the litter. Each time, the littlest one got up and forced her way back to the bowl of kibble. "She's got spunk," I told myself, paraphrasing one of the best-loved lines from *The Mary Tyler Moore Show*. And then she'd be roughly pushed aside by her clan once again. She needed me, and so I put down a deposit.

I named her Billie (after Billie Holiday, the jazz singer, who faced much adversity), and once home my pup displayed spunk in spades. On hot summer days, I'd throw a tennis ball into our pool and she'd leap into the water—paws akimbo—then dog-paddle to the steps and climb out, grinning (yes, I swear, grinning). She'd then shake herself dry, that clipped tail furiously wagging, drenching me and David—my housemate and friend, and Billie's other dog dad—in the process. No matter.

Billie was also peripatetic, in epic proportions. Over her lifetime, she obtained elite status on United, having flown miles and miles in the friendly skies. On one occasion, airline personnel left her behind on the tarmac, in her crate, and then called me to say, "Your dog missed its connection." When she finally arrived, more than six hours later, I was a mess; she, all kisses.

And she was smart: able to open doors with a single paw.

I didn't fully understand then what science would confirm decades later: Billie had not only spunk, but an amazing ability to boost my mood. Little by little she started to nose me out of my cancer funk.

"Study after study has shown that owning a pet can help you maintain a more positive, optimistic perspective on life and what you're faced with," Susanna Newsonen, a writer and philosopher, writes in *Psychology Today*. "Better yet, they can even lessen the symptoms of depression and anxiety." Jane Manno, a Cleveland Clinic psychologist who conducted a study on the impact four-leggeds have on us two-leggeds, reports that "just physically, being around animals releases some positive neurotransmitters in the brain." She's referencing serotonin and dopamine, which make us feel good and even lower blood pressure and decrease levels of the stress hormone cortisol.

Less scientific, but not necessarily less valid, many dog owners attest that getting out of the house to walk their pooches, having a dog curl up next to them, and being responsible for a pup's day-to-day care simply make them feel better. "There is just something magic about dogs," a Brit told *The Guardian*, referencing his small rescue dog named Maria. A social worker agreed, telling the newspaper, "Dogs love us unconditionally. They're the ultimate in equal opportunities—entirely indifferent to race, gender, star sign, CV, clothes size or ability to throw cool moves on the dance floor. The simplicity and depth of this love is a continuous joy."

Fast-forward a decade, with that puppy now a grand old dame. One evening after dinner, I didn't find Billie in her cozy bed. Instead, she'd taken refuge in the living room, fretfully pawing at her right eye as though she had a painful headache. I approached—on my knees—to see what the problem might be. One quick look and I saw trouble: her right eye, usually hazel-brown, had clouded over; it was nearly opaque. An emergency call to the vet only heightened my anxiety. "Bring her in first thing," he told me.

It was already too late. "Acute glaucoma," he explained the next morning. "Her optic nerve has been crushed. She's now permanently blind in that eye." Seeing my distress, he made a point of saying: "Dogs are very resilient. Before you know it, she'll have made an accommodation for her lost sight." Of course, some dogs are more resilient than others, just like us two-leggeds. Those of us with greater resilience—to a setback, an illness, or a tragedy—can recover more easily than those who may dwell on their loss for months, even years.

Amazingly, Billie did just fine, deftly navigating the house and even new hiking trails. She embraced each day as new—sniff, sniff, sniff!—without any sense of what might have been lost. I wish I could have been that resilient. Despite my progress, I remained tangled up in cancer fear and anxiety, and what I considered to have been taken from me: a sense of innocence and invulnerability.

A year after Billie lost vision in one eye, I watched her clamber out of her bed one morning and walk right into the bedroom door. The next day she tumbled down a short flight of stairs (thankfully, carpeted). She couldn't find her water bowl (but she did sniff out her food bowl). Despite my attentiveness to her health, with not just regular checkups but also daily eye drops, the vet confirmed that she was now blind in both eyes. The cause this time: a detached retina. "There's no chance for recovery," he explained, again reminding David and me that "a dog is tenacious in the face of adversity." He also added that she'd remain "happy and boisterous," clear proxies for joyful.

His prophesy about her resilience turned out to be right. After a few days, Billie began what I considered a spectacular adjustment to a sightless world, first tentatively roaming from room to room, then venturing up and down the stairs. Eventually David and I took her on hikes in the Berkeley foothills, keeping her on leash as our only concession to her blindness. More to the point, her clipped tail wagged incessantly. Unlike me, even in adversity Billie didn't miss a beat or lose her joyful bounce and pounce. I took note.

I watched Billie experience joy from within. From memory. From her other senses, especially her sense of smell. It no longer seemed to come from an external source like a bouncing ball, the sight of a horse, or a taunting squirrel. I loved how our cocker spaniel, "the runt with spunk," as I often referred to her, spread an infectious exuberance to David and me, our families and friends. (Long after she died from a stomach cancer, we still remember and recount her many antics—leaping into the pool, scarfing six burgers behind our backs, refusing to give up a slice of pizza despite both bribes and threats.)

There proved to be deeper lessons as well.

Danielle Casioppo, a staff member of Being Well at Yale, has studied and written about the challenge of cultivating joy from within. She notes that many people think of joy "as originating from or being caused by an external stimulus, such as rejoicing about something spiritual or a fortuitous occurrence." Our traditions, she laments, "do not explicitly instruct on how to cultivate joy from within, on one's own."

Her point: if we can give ourselves the tools to cultivate joy, we can learn to feel more joyful on our own, instead of waiting for some sort of external "thing" that has to precede that joyful feeling. With no disrespect to the Yale researchers, I think it's fair to say Billie figured this out years before they did. A dog is the living embodiment of joy, one that is innate, and usually contagious.

Casioppo and I talked for a long time on the phone one cold winter's day, I with my new pup (yes, another cocker spaniel) on my lap, she with her fourteen-year-old rescue named Louie at her feet. "I adopted him from the animal shelter I used to volunteer at because I was one of the only people he trusted," she told me. "He was having a very hard time being adopted and was on the list for euthanasia. He stole my heart and has been a temperamental little joy since then." She laughed. I laughed. I understood. I moved on, asking, "Do you think that many people have a hard time recognizing joy, much less experiencing it?"

"I would say that joy is always there. It's always available to us," she began. "We just need to be open to it. It doesn't mean that we have to live our life 24/7 feeling joyful—ecstatic and wonderfully content—because, of course, that's not realistic. But it's possible to allow ourselves momentary glimpses and touchpoints of joy. . . . It is just a matter of choice."

Always the skeptic, I asked her for an example. Without missing a beat, she told me that she'd recently gone to a trampoline park with her eight-year-old daughter. Most of the other parents sat around talking, maybe watching their kids jump out of the corners of their eyes, but Giovanna implored her, "Please, you have to come jump with me!" Casioppo, then forty-seven, did just that. "We had such a good time," she told me. "It was so much fun. I was laughing and felt like a little kid. There was so much joy between the two of us and it was kind of an exuberant, excited, just gleeful type of joy that I hadn't felt to that degree in a while."

Like many of us, Casioppo is weighed down by various stresses—from the economy to climate change to political polarization, as well as being a mom who has long suffered from depression. "There's always something," she said, sounding a bit like *Saturday Night Live*'s Roseanne Roseannadanna (a.k.a. the late Gilda Radner). That doesn't mean we can't find joy within, she said, noting that family, friends, pets—even nature and music—can all help activate it. On those days or weeks when we feel there's nothing to be joyful about, she reminds me that we still have the choice to be joyful for others when they're doing well. That's what's known as vicarious joy, she added.

Casioppo's words stayed with me. "We still have the choice. . . ." Put another way, it's like the T-shirt a friend wears and I covet, "I Choose Joy."

As for my Billie, our story wound up taking a pretty big turn. One afternoon, after she'd been blind in both eyes for most of a year, I inadvertently kicked a tennis ball across the living room. In a flash she ran after it, grabbed it with her mouth, and returned grinning, reminding me of her early ball-fetching days at our pool. "It's amazing how her other senses have heightened to compensate for her lost vision," I told David on the phone that evening. "Our dog is a genius!" he replied.

A few days later, with Billie back at David's house across the Bay, he phoned me, his voice full of excitement: "Remember the magnolia tree out in the backyard? The branches have grown so close to the house that any critter can basically walk in the sunroom window. . . ." He yammered on with dual lessons in horticulture and patio design. "Get to the point!" I pleaded. "Okay, okay," he replied, moving on with the tale. "I was bringing Billie upstairs when I saw this raccoon on the window ledge. Billie saw it, too, and just took off like a bullet toward it. This dog is clearly not blind," David said, finally making his point.

"No, no, no," came our vet's response when I called. He suggested we were suffering from wishful thinking, if not a delusional fantasy.

I insisted on an in-person visit, arriving to find the office decked out for Christmas—with the tree anchored to the floor and with not a single strand of tinsel or lights, but covered with a slew of handmade paper ornaments, each with a message like "Don't argue with a vet, they know how to neuter" and "It's all fun and games until someone winds up in a cone." And how could I forget the tailored Muzak loop, featuring classics like "Grandma Got Run Over by a Reindeer" and the hilarious "I Want a Hippopotamus for Christmas."

After examining Billie, the vet returned to the waiting room; there were tears in his eyes as he spoke to David and me. "This happens so rarely, but the retina has spontaneously reattached. This is a Christmas miracle." He'd read about retinas reattaching, he told us, but in all his years of practice he had never witnessed it.

Was it really a miracle? I don't know, but what I do know is this: there's much in this world that science still can't explain. In the days before modern medicine, before knowledge overshadowed faith, it was common for talismans and amulets (objects believed to have magical powers) to have their place in any self-respecting doctor's bag. It's much easier to rationalize, minimize, or plain forget about the joy of a possible miracle. Instead, I prefer to marvel at Billie's outcome.

This also led to some changes in my mindset, even softening my jaundiced view of those classic Christmas films. "Faith is believing things when common sense tells you not to," declares Fred Gailey, a lawyer in *Miracle on 34th Street* who defies reason in his determination to prove that Santa Claus exists. "Don't you see? It's not just Kris [Kringle] that's on trial, it's everything he stands for. It's kindness and joy and love and all the other intangibles."

As for sweet Billie, she lived for several more years, passing away in 2009, the day after I'd decorated the Christmas tree. To this day, an ornament bearing her likeness sits atop the tree, reminding me to believe.

## How to Believe in Magic

When I was first diagnosed with cancer in my mid-twenties, I read every evidence-based, peer-reviewed study I could get my hands on so I could make the best-informed treatment decisions. My odds of survival were actually pretty decent, but I found that data insufficient. Put simply: science could not guarantee me a 100 percent successful outcome.

Not long after my diagnosis, my friend Cynthia gave me a velvety rabbit with big floppy ears, a silver tiara, and a name tag that read "Fairy God Bunny." Cynthia insisted that the bunny had "magical powers," which she boosted by later adding a wand trimmed in gold lamé. That bunny was intended to be my talisman, a magical defender against my cancer. For five years I carried this rabbit with me to the hospital for labs, CT scans, and X-rays, even though I was a twenty-six-year-old Ph.D. candidate.

In an interview, Stuart Vyse, a psychologist and the author of *Believing in Magic*, told me that many people turn to "irrational beliefs" in times of dire need. Whenever medical science does not provide a cure, there's going to be a "psychological gap, the need of something better," he said. "It's not uncommon to be of two minds and to say, 'I know this is crazy, but I'll feel better if I do it anyway.'" (Let me add that the good psychologist's take-home message is about the importance of following the path of evidence, science, and reason.)

So, how can we both adhere to the scientific method and incorporate a sense of magic or wonder into our lives?

First, understand there is no real "magic" that can change objective facts, but rituals and superstitions have been shown to affect mood and even performance on certain tasks. The ritual itself doesn't matter, but the reduced anxiety that comes with completing a ritual—any ritual—helps many people to feel better. So if you have some version of a fairy god bunny, go ahead and use it. Rub its ears, poke its belly, whatever it is you do before an important test or performance. It may just improve your mood and help you perform better.

Second, understand that self-deception has conferred evolutionary benefits on us. Embrace those self-deceptions, even as you recognize them for what they are. The horseshoe hung over your doorway won't actually bring good luck, and that image of St. Christopher, the patron saint of travelers, won't actually protect against car wrecks. But if you feel better relying on such beliefs, why not? (Provided you lock your doors and keep fresh batteries in the smoke detectors, that is.)

# THE JOY OF BEING SINGLE

I love Chelsea Handler, the unofficial spokesperson of singles everywhere.

Actually, I was late to find Handler's comedy, as I was late to her full-throttled embrace of singledom. Once I started following her work, however, I couldn't stop. She erased any vestige of personal failure remaining from my divorce. She obliterated my shame. She is my joy.

One of my favorite things to watch is a TikTok where Handler finds herself at home, alone, eating take-out Thai on a TV tray.

"Don't mind me, I was just having a little snack," she begins her monologue, wearing a white cashmere sweater, her tone completely earnest. "See, I was craving Thai food, so I ordered Thai food," she continues on, surrounded by at least seven white cartons from her local take-out Thai place. "Pretty crazy, right? I can do that sort of thing because I'm not married. I didn't have to politely ask my husband, 'What do you want to eat tonight, honey?' And have him say, 'I don't know, what do you want to eat?' And then I say, 'How about some Thai food?' And then he complains, 'I hate Thai food. We always get Thai food. . . .' [Now] I can eat whatever I want, whenever I want."

Six springs ago, I officially joined the singles crowd when my ex-husband forwarded an email from his attorney with the subject line "You are DIVORCED!" I'll admit it seemed excessively jubilant, especially in light of the harshness of the final decree, which read: "The bonds of matrimony which have existed between the parties are dissolved and the plaintiff is granted an absolute divorce from the defendant."

There I was at age sixty, yet again identified as—take your pick—solo, unmarried, unattached, unwed, or alone. No matter what anyone called it, I was *single*. When I bought my post-divorce house, the title company listed me as "a single man," which felt like a badge of shame, a red letter "S" (for Steven and Single) affixed to my chest. No matter where I turned, I couldn't avoid the question: "What is your marital status?" It leered at me from my medical chart, financial disclosure forms, Social Security documents, loan and credit applications, a new health club registration, marketing questionnaires, certain vital records, the U.S. Census, and—no surprise—online dating apps (where I've learned a good percentage of men lie about everything from their marital status to their height, weight, and most of all, age).

As if that weren't sufficient, there always comes the inevitable next question: "Why?" As in: "Why are you single?" (Something no one should ever ask.) Implicit in that seemingly simple query is a more odious one: "What's the matter with you?" Look, I'd not expected to be single as a sexagenarian; actually, I believed what we'd recited in our marriage vows. (You know the line, "Until death do us part.") My answer to long-term care insurance or whether to sign up for a retirement community? A husband. Ditto when it came to a travel companion or someone to share household expenses. "We live in a culture that tends to celebrate and exalt couples," writes Catherine Gray in *The Unexpected Joy of Being Single*, "but pigeonholes singles as outliers, misfits, oddballs who can't find someone to love them."

Of course, there are other fail-safes that are now no more. Who to ferry me to the doctor in an emergency, who to help with buying a house, and who to go to bed with on a regular—even irregular—basis? Still, I can eat whatever I want whenever I want.

I've learned a lot since those early days of my newly single life. It's easy to feel alone when you're single. But we're not. The U.S. Census Bureau reports that more than 126 million Americans age eighteen and older are single, a number that's growing. There's a distinction between being alone and being lonely, and I admit I'm exuberantly happy not to share a bathroom and a bed, or to be in a relationship that included my mother-in-law, echoing what the late Princess Diana once bemoaned, "There were three of us in the marriage."

As it turns out, new studies are shedding fresh light on that old myth about marrieds being healthier and happier. In fact, unmarried people—singles!—tend to enjoy greater health and well-being than their partnered counterparts. If you're unpartnered, you're much more likely to exercise regularly (even if, or because, you're doing it to keep in shape to attract someone new). Single women have been found to have lower BMIs and fewer risks associated with smoking and alcohol than married women, according to a study published in the *Journal of Women's Health*. Oh, and this should come as no surprise: singles have sex more often than married people, and more sex is associated with greater well-being or joy.

In fact, single, child-free women are the happiest of all demographics, according to Paul Dolan, a professor of behavioral science at the prestigious London School of Economics and the author of *Happy Ever After*. He attributes their joy, in part, to extremely strong friendships, while a study published in the *Journal of Social and Personal Relationships* concludes that being single boosts social connections because uncoupled people are more likely to rely on their social and professional networks than their married or partnered friends. Yep, that sounds about right.

Still, as I approached sixty, two specific fears kept me awake at night and anxious by day. How would I celebrate this milestone birthday? My parents had thrown my fiftieth celebration; I'd expected my husband to do the honors this time around. When two couples in my small town realized I had no plans, they asked if they could throw me a party. I replied yes, which honestly wasn't so easy, because it required a big mind shift—to lean into my friendships. On the other hand, I had no plan B.

The first clue to what awaited me arrived in my inbox. The invitation boasted a fiery wreath. The theme: Disco Inferno. Red and white attire was suggested, plus "a heated spirit." The night of the party, I arrived in my friends' backyard, only to be greeted by a life-size cardboard cutout of . . . me!

The organizing committee had taken it up a notch further, rewriting the lyrics of "Hello, Dolly!" to "Hello, Petrow!" which a dozen friends sang to me as I joyfully wept. In a short speech, I confessed to everyone that my marital separation had left me fearful of two things: what to do on this birthday (check), and who would drive me to my next colonoscopy (a friend raised his hand at that very moment). A day that I had dreaded became one of the most beautiful evenings I'd experienced, thanks to these friends who were becoming my family of choice. Perhaps single wasn't so bad after all.

Jamie Daniel-Farrell, who specializes in marriage counseling and what she calls "divorce recovery," noted much the same in her personal and professional life, writing, "If you're brave enough to let your story be known, others going through a similar experience will come out of the woodwork and be drawn to you. Genuinely supportive friendships can form." This, she said, can help with feelings of loneliness and isolation, and I say it can change your life.

I wondered what other joys people found in being unattached, so, naturally, I asked friends on Facebook. I sure got an earful.

"I don't have to shave my legs if I don't want to."

"I can play whatever music I want."

"No more sharing the ice cream or the Oreos or worrying who gets the last bite of peanut butter from the Skippy jar."

"I can drink milk out of the carton and not worry about getting caught."

"Sleeping on either side of the bed—or even sideways."

"Traveling the world with friends."

"Not worrying about my partner snoring and not caring whether I do."

"No one to answer to about money."

"A body pillow that doesn't complain about being hugged."

"I can play the piano at six in the morning."

"No more negotiation over what to watch on TV."

"No more bickering."

"Not having to cook dinner even if it's my turn."

"Not having to pull someone else's hair out of the drain."

"Not being judged."

But the winner of the People's Choice Award for being single—"No more worrying about shamelessly exuberant flatulence." (Yes, more people listed unrepentant farting as an answer than anything else.)

I'm not arguing that it's necessarily better to be single than partnered or married (although I know my friend Chelsea Handler thinks that). But half a decade after my divorce (and still single), I get to eat what I want, when I want; I decide where to put the art in my house; and my vacations are no longer a ménage à trois. I love what Catherine Gray writes: "Singles are not half people, we are full people, and perfectly complete the way we are."

I've also rediscovered two of my greatest joys, tennis and canoeing, which conveniently reminds me of what the never-married Louisa May Alcott once famously wrote: "I'd rather be a free spinster and paddle my own canoe."

## How to Be Joyfully, Shamelessly, Unapologetically Single

No matter how many messages bombard us about how everyone's happiness depends on being paired off, that is simply not the case. Many of us are living happy and fulfilling lives without romantic partners, thank you very much. Experts agree that the single life can be a satisfying and complete one, assuming we make finding joy a priority. Here are some strategies that will help you tune out the not-so-helpful questions and advice, and instead focus on finding the joy in being one—with yourself, with the universe, with a pet, or whatever brings you joy.

**Stay connected.** Being single doesn't mean being a hermit—it's still important for health and happiness to feel connected to others. According to the Mayo Clinic, friendships play a large role in promoting overall health. Having friends reduces the risk of depression, high blood pressure, and obesity, and older adults with strong social connections live longer than those without. So if you feel yourself starting to slip from happily single to sad and lonely, make a conscious effort to reconnect with friends, family members, colleagues, and others.

**Take yourself on dates.** Too often we forgo special outings and events because they seem like "date night" occasions. They don't have to be! Think about where you might want to go on a date and go on your own. As Anne Posey, a licensed mental health counselor, said in an interview with the Cleveland Clinic, "Doing the things we enjoy or exploring our passions is a very positive pastime. You aren't required to be in a relationship to live life!" Posey encourages singles to do the things that interest them, without waiting for a date. "Make a list of things you want to try and go do them," she added. "You can sit home and mope about being single, or you can be single and do things you enjoy."

**Get to know thyself.** Whether your single status is a temporary hiatus or a long-term plan, it's an excellent time for introspection. Without the protective veneer we often put on around others, we can be truly honest about our strengths and weaknesses. "Being single makes room for a person to learn more about themselves," psychotherapist Babita Spinelli told the MindBodyGreen website. "There is more clarity around who you are and leaning into enjoying your own company."

**Use (all) the space.** One of the compromises of partnered life is shared space—nobody wants to see your socks on the floor, and you don't need someone else's dishes in the sink. Having a partner takes up mental space as well—when did he say he was going to the doctor, and did she remember to pay that credit card bill? One of the great joys of the solo life is that all the space is yours—all of it, literally and figuratively.

**Enjoy your freedom.** No explanation needed.

# THE JOY OF A DANCE PARTY

Between Halloween and Thanksgiving, I found myself dragging in familiar ways. I didn't want to get out of bed, and then I couldn't wait to take a midmorning nap. This was the third pandemic fall. At this point in my life, I knew the telltale signs of depression—specifically inertia, sluggishness, overeating, and a shortened fuse. Close friends could also see the dark cloud looming over me, and a few suggested I try to remember what I'd done to shake off previous glooms. More exercise. Less drinking. Better sleep. Then my friend Vince asked me this straightforward question: "What has brought you joy in the past that you're not doing now?"

I didn't have a ready answer. (Only later did I realize I'd halted my early morning sing-a-thon. Call it Ethel Merman meets Julie Andrews because, while walking outside, dog in tow, I'd belt out round after round of "Do-Re-Mi" from *The Sound of Music.* I kept going until either I couldn't breathe anymore, or I encountered a neighbor.) A few weeks after Vince posed his question, my friends Ashley and Peter invited a dozen of us to a dance party at their house in the woods.

Their invitation to a dance party reminded me of when I went to my first gay club almost fifty years ago. There, I'd met a handsome fellow named Bill, lean and lithe with a mop of curly hair. As soon as the first familiar notes of The Supremes' hit "I Hear a Symphony" filled the house, Bill asked me onto the dance floor, where we cut a rug for hours on end, swirling and sweating, before kissing—a joyful explosion detonating within me. Even now, my body remains imprinted with the euphoria of that evening.

Ashley and Peter's email invitation, written in lavender script, spoke to our deep isolation and deskbound lives.

*It has been a difficult time, for several years,*
*and for many reasons, some global, some close*
*to home. In the spirit of togetherness*
*and healing, let's dance.*

And dance we did—on their screened porch, a disco ball shimmering above, the fog machine on full blast, a strobe running through the colors of the rainbow. I felt like my nineteen-year-old self again, cocooned among a sea of bodies, swaying and stepping, twirling and turning. By the time the first set ended, I was gasping for breath as I ran my hand through my soaking wet hair. I'd lost track of the time. Call it fun, call it joy, I don't care, but we danced the night away.

Toni Bergins, who teaches JourneyDance classes at Kripalu, the wellness retreat in the Berkshires, said, "Everyone has their own definition of fun, but one key to fun is that time flies by. You're so into it that you don't even know what's happening." Exactly!

Sure, part of my elation was how the music—Diana Ross, Tina Turner, and Gloria Gaynor—streaming from the speakers evoked happy memories of days gone by. This kind of experience—when music helps retrieve long-ago memories of people, places, and events—is actually quite common and a subject of study. It's known as music-evoked autobiographical memory, which means that music has a unique capacity to evoke both strong emotions and vivid autobiographical memories, according to a 2021 study. For me, that song by The Supremes always triggers a remembrance of that first kiss with Bill, the sweet touch of our lips . . . before we headed to my place for the night. But I realized there were other dimensions to my joy as well.

Thanks to the pandemic, the mere act of being in a group of people had become infrequent, for a while almost nonexistent. I'd stopped going to Spin class at my gym, where my energy fed off of "competitors" and a good song list. Conferences had become virtual, no longer allowing for spontaneous conversations. We had no more concerts, plays, or dance performances. We humans crave that shared euphoria—and I didn't realize how much I'd missed it until I stepped out on Ashley and Peter's screened porch turned dance floor.

In the early twentieth century, French sociologist Émile Durkheim coined the term "collective effervescence," which refers to the heightened sense of self-transcendence people feel when they come together for a shared purpose. He considered it a key component of how we can better cope with the vicissitudes of life. Adam Grant, an organizational psychologist, puts it more colloquially in a recent essay: "It's a concept . . . to describe the sense of energy and harmony people feel when they come together in a group around a shared purpose." If Durkheim were alive today, I'm certain he'd point to any of Taylor Swift's or Beyoncé's concerts as a contemporary example of his theory. Or the New York Jets. My brother has experienced what he describes as a "fanatical" sense of connection and pride to his beloved team, win or lose, for half a century.

"The neurochemistry that makes moving in unison euphoric also bonds strangers and builds trust," writes psychologist Kelly McGonigal, author of *The Joy of Movement*. "This is why moving together is one of the ways humans come together. Collective action reminds us what we are part of, and moving in community reminds us where we belong," she adds.

I hadn't been fully aware of what I'd been missing during Covid—that is, until we all started stepping out again. Recent research has found that we're likely to laugh five times as often when we're with others than when we're alone, sparking both delight and joy. But it's movement that can produce euphoria, which became palpable on the dance floor.

Movement—or exercise—is well documented to help with depression. "In people who are depressed, neuroscientists have noticed that the hippocampus in the brain—the region that helps regulate mood—is smaller," explained Michael Craig Miller, an assistant professor of psychiatry at Harvard Medical School, in an interview with Harvard Health Publishing. "Exercise supports nerve cell growth in the hippocampus, improving nerve cell connections, which helps relieve depression," he added.

Music, too, can lessen the impacts of depression and anxiety, and create a deeper sense of community/connection, according to studies. When I think about Gloria Gaynor, best known for the 1970s disco hit "I Will Survive," I recall not only the pulsing beat but its underlying message of personal empowerment and resilience, just the shot of joy I can always count on to find my way out of the darkness.

## Let's Plan a Dance Party Playlist!

Like any event, a dance party can be as simple or elaborate as you like. Sure there's lighting, drinks, snacks, and maybe a theme—but none of that comes close to matching the main event, which is simply the music.

If you're like me, you probably have a special place in your heart for the music of your youth, which is my way of admitting my playlist is biased toward the dance tunes of the 1970s and '80s. I know my twentysomething nieces have their own attachments. No matter, the best dance music transcends time and generations. A pulsing bass line, driving beat, memorable lyrics—it's the perfect recipe for a can't-miss dance hit. The following thirty songs are favorites of mine. Use them. Lose them. But get up and dance.

1. "Dancing Queen," ABBA, 1976
2. "You Make Me Feel (Mighty Real)," Sylvester, 1978
3. "Y.M.C.A.," Village People, 1978
4. "Got to Be Real," Cheryl Lynn, 1978
5. "Last Dance," Donna Summer, 1978
6. "I Will Survive," Gloria Gaynor, 1978
7. "Good Times," Chic, 1979
8. "Don't Stop 'til You Get Enough," Michael Jackson, 1979

9. "We Are Family," Sister Sledge, 1979
10. "I'm Coming Out," Diana Ross, 1980
11. "It's Raining Men," The Weather Girls, 1982
12. "1999," Prince, 1982
13. "Gloria," Laura Ann Branigan, 1982
14. "Move Your Body (The House Music Anthem)," Marshall Jefferson, 1986
15. "Push It," Salt-N-Pepa, 1986
16. "I Wanna Dance with Somebody (Who Loves Me)," Whitney Houston, 1987
17. "Vogue," Madonna, 1990
18. "U Can't Touch This," MC Hammer, 1990
19. "Finally," CeCe Peniston, 1991
20. "Show Me Love," Robin S., 1993
21. "Believe," Cher, 1998
22. "Get Ur Freak On," Missy Elliott, 2001
23. "Crazy in Love," Beyoncé featuring Jay-Z, 2003
24. "I Gotta Feeling," Black Eyed Peas, 2009
25. "Born This Way," Lady Gaga, 2011
26. "Turn Down for What," DJ Snake featuring Lil Jon, 2013
27. "Shake It Off," Taylor Swift, 2014
28. "Uptown Funk," Mark Ronson featuring Bruno Mars, 2014
29. "Don't Start Now," Dua Lipa, 2019
30. "Texas Hold 'Em," Beyoncé, 2024

# THE JOY OF THE MUNDANE

For most of my life, I hated undertaking home tasks. I did not like housecleaning, washing my car, or doing the dishes, much less the laundry.

I found these activities boring, at best. A time waste, at worst. But one day, a friend lent me her copy of *The Miracle of Mindfulness* by the Buddhist monk Thích Nhất Hạnh. Of the 140-some pages, I hyperfocused on a specific passage about washing dishes:

> If while washing dishes, we think only of the cup of tea that awaits us, thus hurrying to get the dishes out of the way as if they were a nuisance . . . then we are not alive during the time we are washing the dishes. In fact we are completely incapable of realizing the miracle of life while standing at the sink. If we can't wash the dishes, the chances are we won't be able to drink our tea either.

Oh please, this guy doesn't have a clue, even if he is a famous monk, I thought to myself. For so many years, my mother, a disciple of Betty Friedan, could not wait for the day when we would be able to afford a dishwasher (other than herself, that is). She believed that housework, including cooking and cleaning, was pure drudgery, fronting as a form of patriarchal oppression.

In many ways I'm like my mother. While I can't claim that I'm a victim of the patriarchy when I take care of the house, I'm always on the hunt for shortcuts to life's tedious tasks. Just this past summer I bought a Eufy RoboVac, one of those new robot vacuums, which promises to "turn chore time into play time!" Eufy efficiently crawled through the house scarfing dust balls, dead bugs, and dog hair. That is, until it reached the top of a staircase and launched right off, tumbling to the bottom, looking like it had chosen its own destruction over another day of mundanity.

Mundanity, it turns out, gets a bad rap; it's really only drudgery if you choose to see chores in that light. That's not just me speaking. In recent years, researchers have been focused on why mundane moments truly matter. For example, Ting Zhang, an assistant professor at Harvard Business School, told *The New York Times* at the outset of the pandemic that "people underestimate the value of documenting the present, especially the mundane. We hire photographers for special occasions, but don't really capture the rich day-to-day experiences that make up so much of our life."

To that point, I've always appreciated Annie Dillard's caution that "how we spend our days is how we spend our lives," which is another way of explaining the importance of what can be revealed by valuing, if not recording, the ordinary. My friend, the photographer Tom Rankin, regularly posts photographs from his day-to-day life. At the top of his Facebook feed recently: three parked cars bathed in the morning light; Rudolph, the red-nosed reindeer, gracing a tree in his front yard; and the three beautiful dogs he shares with his wife, Jill—Blue, Frankie, and Lena. As Tom told me, "What else is there but the mundane, the ordinary, the quotidian?"

I decided to embark on an experiment in seeking joy in the mundane. I began with dishwashing. Rather than seeing it as drudgery, I tried to see it as an opportunity. It allowed me to spend ten, fifteen, or thirty minutes doing nothing in a sense, which has its own virtues. I found it to be a gift of time, allowing my mind to wander, which a friend describes as "mind emptying."

Standing before the kitchen sink, I deliberately rinse off plates, glasses, knives, and forks, and then wash them carefully with a soapy sponge, finally completing another rinse before carefully placing each item on the drying rack. I feel the warmth of the water and the slipperiness of the suds, which is comforting, akin to being in a bath. There's also a slight sense of danger—what if I break a dish? More than anything, there's a sense of satisfaction that comes with completing the dishes by myself. Surprisingly, it actually helps to ease my monkey mind and to make me more present.

One friend described a similar experience in washing and folding her clothes, which you may think is too much. But it's genuine, which, like gratitude, is part of the recipe for joy.

> I feel such joy in doing laundry! Joy that I have a place in my home to do it. Joy that I have things to wash and people to wash it for. Joy when I have extra loads of towels and sheets because it means we had friends stay over. I also remind myself that not everyone has clean water to wash clothes.

There's also something uncommon that takes place in performing these activities: finishing—completely finishing—what we set out to do. These short-term tasks give us a framework, and by that I mean a beginning, middle, and end. How often do we start and complete a task or a project in daily life? I don't, that's for sure.

I especially like that there's often no thinking required; it's a habit that resurrects spontaneously, and can even remind us of times past. Before my mother got her much-coveted dishwasher, my brother, sister, and I took regular turns on kitchen patrol, playfully arguing with each other about who would scrape, wash, or rinse. Although we protested too much, I remember those times as filled with laughter, ribbing, and the occasional broken glass. These days when I wash dishes, I sometimes take flight to my childhood, happily recalling those memories.

On one New Year's Eve several years ago, I hosted eight friends for dinner, serving the salad, soup, and entrée on my grandmother's Wedgwood china. (If I remember the story correctly, this set of dinnerware had been a gift at Grandma Marjorie's wedding to my grandfather in 1927.) Although the laurel leaf at the center of the plates is now faded (with some of the dishes cracked and chipped), the memories of oxtail stew dinners served on those very plates remain intact. Naturally, I couldn't use my dishwasher for Grandma's china, which meant doing them by hand. That moment reconnected me with the past, which blended seamlessly back to the present. I wanted to be careful, so did not rush. Instead, I felt a deliberate stillness or calmness. I was paying attention in a way I rarely did (to just about anything), and I developed a rhythm, a flow—like a slow dancer—as I washed, rinsed, and dried. "Doing the dishes is a time for clarity and both literal and figurative digestion," writes Charlotte Muru-Lanning in "The Art of Washing Dishes."

I've also extended the practice of appreciating the mundane to other daily activities—making the bed, food shopping, tending to my garden—as a way to be "here" and not "there." Did I mention the delight I experience in completing a task? It's a joy I can relive every single day, that is, if I make my bed on a daily basis.

As I finish up the dishes, usually with Chet Baker or Billie Holiday streaming in the background, I'm aware that I've been in a liminal space, one between being and not being, one where all is possible, one where I am grateful, content, and satisfied; one where there's a modicum of order in a world that often seems out of control. If I'm lucky, as I take out the trash, I'll see the silhouetted trees across the street from me dancing against the navy-blue velvet of the night. A moment of magic, thanks to my cutting, cleaning, chopping, and cooking.

## How to Practice the Art of Washing Dishes

When an internationally renowned Buddhist monk (Thích Nhất Hạnh) and an emerging New Zealand writer (Charlotte Muru-Lanning) both extol the joy of the same mundane task, I pay attention. Nhất Hạnh, who died in 2022, took an elevated perspective on practicing mindfulness during everyday chores, mentioning washing dishes in particular. Muru-Lanning took that to a new level, even including a ten-step how-to guide on the details of dishwashing.

Where Nhất Hạnh wrote about the exquisite attention he paid to the tactile sensations, the in-the-moment experience of his hands in the water, Muru-Lanning is hands-on and no-nonsense. She has specific advice on what to use (not those "annoying" dish brushes, but a scrubby cloth—her favorite is a Korean crochet dish sponge) and how to proceed (cleanest items first, get those suds rinsed off, air-dry upside down in a good-quality dish rack). As she puts it, "Handwashing the dishes can be a beautiful synergy of organic flow if done right."

For Muru-Lanning, handwashing is about more than just finding "solace in the mundane," although that's part of it. She writes that she thinks of it as part of the larger experience of preparing and sharing meals. Much has been written about the joys of communal dining, less about the cleanup. But "if a meal were a film," Muru-Lanning writes, "dishes would be the final scene."

So if you think of doing dishes as drudgery, try to take a different perspective next time you approach the sink. Muru-Lanning's guide is strong on quality—her suggestion about swapping out your cheap drying towels for good ones is a subtle way to boost your task and give it the respect it deserves in your day—and self-care (protecting your hands and using moisturizer after the job is done), a reminder of how important *you* are, which I'm on board with 100 percent.

# THE JOY OF READING

In the winter of 1973, which was eleventh grade for me, I chose an English class that included a formidable roster of authors so famous that they didn't need first names—Shakespeare, Wordsworth, Milton, Molière, Hawthorne, Irving, Thoreau, and Melville. Our teacher, Mr. Neumeier, a single, well-built man in his forties who sported muscle T-shirts and a Walt Whitman–style beard, appeared as imposing to me as any of the writers on our syllabus.

What I remember most about that class is Mr. Neumeier's enthusiasm for reading in general, and for "Hermie" (his nickname for Melville) in particular. Standing before us on that first day, a motley crew of teens from the five boroughs of New York, he spoke so softly that I remember craning my neck to hear him emphasize how reading would allow us to time travel, globe-trot, and meet new friends and foes. I recall he said something like, "You're going to experience lives completely unlike your own. Fasten your seat belts."

That year, I traveled to Scotland in the early 1600s, took up residence on a whaler off the New England coast in the mid-eighteenth century, and found myself visiting the Massachusetts Bay Colony in the mid-seventeenth century. I met Lady Macbeth, Captain Ahab, and Hester Prynne.

I'd become a voracious reader by then, wanting to escape the ordinariness of daily life and find comfort with others who might better understand me. I'm remembering specifically the protagonist Carol Milford in Sinclair Lewis's bestselling novel *Main Street*, who remains an outsider and social outcast despite marrying the local doctor. I understood her isolation. As for the characters in Mr. Neumeier's readings, I didn't find much, if anything, in common with most of them. Still, by spending time with them on the page, I came to know them, even to imagine what their lives must be like. Despite the madness, brutality, and overarching ambition, I slowly developed the ability to understand their worlds from their perspective, even to infer their beliefs and intentions. I didn't understand it at the time, but Mr. Neumeier was teaching a class about empathy, defined as "the ability to understand and share the feelings of another."

Put another way, we read to know that we're not alone.*

One of my favorite social scientists today is Jamil Zaki, an associate professor of psychology at Stanford University and author of *The War for Kindness*, who's written that "fiction is empathy's gate-

*This quote is often attributed to C. S. Lewis, the renowned literary critic. In fact, it's actually from *Shadowlands,* a movie about Lewis.

way drug. It helps us feel for others when real-world caring is too difficult, complicated, or painful." In reading his book, I took note when he explained how "readers can empathize safely even with outsiders they would disavow or avoid in public." More importantly, he said, this kind of interaction on the page can "pave the way for caring about *real* outsiders." Or, as Joyce Carol Oates once noted, "Reading is the sole means by which we slip, involuntarily, often helplessly, into another's skin, another's voice, another's soul."

Meanwhile, numerous researchers have concluded that reading fiction is associated with the development of empathy in both adults and children, providing a scientific underpinning to the important link between the empathy felt for fictional characters (say, Hester Prynne, a woman who scandalously has a child out of wedlock in seventeenth-century Puritan Massachusetts) and the ability to empathize with real people (say, Monica Lewinsky). Why is this important in seeking joy? Well, empathy, it's been noted often, is a fundamental building block to experience joy. In fact, there's even a science of empathetic joy (sometimes referred to as sympathetic joy). A common example is the kind of joy a parent experiences watching their child succeed at school, make new friends, or learn to ride a bicycle.

For me, at sixteen, I delighted in the new worlds and new friends opening up to me, which I can now see taught me to experience the joy of inhabiting someone else's skin, and them, mine.

I unearthed other joys of reading along the way. From time to time, Mr. Neumeier read aloud to us—dramatic readings, always, but I also think he wanted us to get out of our heads, to ensure that we didn't simply become silent, solitary readers. I'd have called myself an introvert in high school, so I struggled when called upon to read a passage aloud to the rest of the class. I can't know how much Mr. Neumeier might have intuited the body of research to come, which we now understand suggests that reading aloud helps improve our memories and boosts our comprehension of complicated texts. Even more important, it strengthens emotional bonds between people. That year, both as listener and reader, I experienced how the classroom held us together. It was as though we were one body, not thirty-five separate cells (yes, we had large classes in the New York City public schools), as though we all belonged to each other. A growing body of research is finding that reading aloud brings joy, comfort, and yes, that very sense of community.

I've continued to read aloud to others throughout my lifetime. My former partner Barry (also a writer) and I loved to end the day in bed, book in hand, as we read to each other before falling asleep in each other's arms. When my mother was ill and no longer able to read, I'd sit by her bedside and read aloud to her, taking my time. Sam Duncan, an adult literacy researcher in the U.K., told the BBC that "when someone is reading aloud to you, you feel a bit like you're given a gift of their time, of their attention, of their voice." We know this with kids; I mean who doesn't love reading to their children, or to their nieces and nephews, and witnessing the connection or bonding that occurs?

We don't do this nearly as much with the adults in our lives. Truth be told, those times with my mom remain among the most beautiful memories I have of her final year. And now, with some distance, I can't help but think that my reading to her reciprocated all that she'd read to me as a child.

One other joy comes to mind as I write this. I fear my other grandmother, Marian the Librarian, would be displeased to hear this confession. "Do not write in the book, Stevie," Grandma reprimanded me often, "especially library books." I mostly obeyed her when it came to borrowed tomes, but once in college, with books that I came to call my own, I started regular conversations with the authors and characters on the printed page. By that, I mean I took my pen to the page, arguing, asking questions, highlighting by underlining, or just scattering exclamation points here and there.

I still have the copy of *Walden* that we read in Mr. Neumeier's class that year. I took on Thoreau in daily missives written in the margins. "My first reaction is to be against everything Thoreau stands for and believes in," I penned on day one. Over the weeks that came after, my marginalia derided Thoreau's "back to nature" perspective as "naïve" and challenged his "innocence" and "purity" as being performative (although I didn't use that word). My intensity, I can see now, belied how personally challenging I found *Walden* and its tenets. Above all, Thoreau's call to authenticity threatened me by threatening to unmask me—as did Mr. Neumeier's lived authenticity. Even then, in an age so closeted, I knew Mr. Neumeier and I had something in common.

By the end of that semester, I'd scribbled on nearly every page of *Walden*. Reading it back as an adult, I see clearly how much I feared removing my mask to know myself, a prerequisite for being known by others. "I spend all too much time trying to hide my true feelings toward people," I wrote one day. A more accurate sentence would have been: "I'm afraid to face the world as I am."

But then something happened. Midpoint in the semester, I can see now, there's a pretty big shift in the tone of my entries. Thoreau's descriptions of Walden began to "sound so beautiful." "The more I think about it I would truly like to tramp through the snow-covered woods of Walden." Not only had I stopped arguing, but I was finding agreement with him. "If we could only act as we truly are, we might be happier and healthier."

I also realized that my empathy for Thoreau was just one part of the equation, as I'd clearly become engaged by Mr. Neumeier himself. I recall the class when he told us, weepily, about a friend of his who'd become seriously ill. My struggle as to what to do or say remains on the page, as does the page I ripped out from my journal and inserted into the book leaves, quoting Kahlil Gibran on sorrow and joy.

My last note in the book, written as we finished the semester, is penned with the cockiness of a teen but still reveals a measure of how far I'd traveled and how much I'd changed. "We have a choice—to continue with our lives as they are now or to wake up. . . . Man cannot hide forever, he alone must set things straight, he must risk himself—"

I'd found my place, the beginnings of community, and a sense of belonging. For me, that has proved to be the ultimate joy of reading.

Three years later, by then in college, I wrote a letter to Mr. Neumeier, outing myself and asking to meet with him. A week later he called me at my parents' house, where I was spending holiday break. He invited me to visit his studio apartment on, yes, Gay Street in the West Village, which I did one snowy winter's day. As we sipped tea from two oversize mugs, he apologized, saying, "I wish I'd been able to be more open with you when you were in my class. I knew you were reaching out." That afternoon, he revealed much more about his own life, from having grown up in a deeply religious family in Escanaba, Michigan, to his life as a gay man in Greenwich Village. He became the friend and mentor I needed then.

A few years later Mr. Neumeier moved to Key West, Florida, after retiring from teaching. In vacating the West Village, he'd taken his books with him, including Melville, Hawthorne, and, of course, Thoreau—"our Thoreau," as I thought of him. In his class, we'd also read a profile of James Baldwin published in a 1963 issue of *Life* magazine, where he says, "You think your pain and your heartbreak are unprecedented in the history of the world, but then you read. It was Dostoevsky and Dickens who taught me that the things that tormented me most were the very things that connected me with all the people who were alive, or who ever had been alive."

Mr. Neumeier—whose full name I finally learned was Charles J. Neumeier—died in Key West at the age of fifty-four. His obituary did not include the cause of death, which was HIV/AIDS. The world was not quite ready for him (or me) in 1985, but we each knew the doom and glory of knowing who we were. I remain grateful to him all these years later, and when I think about him now, I recall what Anne Lamott wrote: "Books . . . show us what community and friendship mean; they show us how to live and die." So, too, teachers. Thank you, Mr. Neumeier.

## How to Make Reading More Joyful

The official statistics tell a sad story about kids: fewer and fewer of them read for pleasure. It's not surprising—getting absorbed in a book used to be the primary way young people learned about other worlds, other times, other people. Today, with all kinds of media available for that, it's not surprising that fewer children want to put the effort into reading. What's even more dispiriting, I think, is how many adults are reading less. A 2022 Gallup poll found that we're reading fewer books a year (this is among adults who do read). A full 17 percent of American adults had not read a single book in the previous year. I get it—we are bombarded with news headlines, videos and reels, websites and apps that are all much less labor-intensive.

**Start small.** Don't try to reignite your love of reading with *War and Peace* or *Finnegans Wake*. Start with short stories or essays. Pick up an anthology or get a trial subscription to *The New Yorker* even if you don't live in the Big Apple—its essays and fiction are world-class.

**Choose topics that interest you.** Don't worry about whether a book is "highbrow" or "lowbrow" or "important" or "serious"—paperback mysteries may be your guilty pleasure, or sci-fi, or romance. I'm not judging! The more you love the topic, the more pleasure you'll get from the experience.

**Identify a regular place or time to do your reading.** I know you can read anywhere, but to fully experience the joy of reading, you can't be waiting in line at the bank or standing over the stove with your Kindle (although when I'm caught up in a page-turner, I'll carry that book everywhere with me). Try to dedicate a certain amount of time a day or a week, pick a comfy chair at home with good lighting, and open your book or fire up your reading device. Then immerse yourself in the words on the page. Don't skim! Don't get distracted, especially if you have wireless connectivity. (If you "read" your books by listening to them, especially if traveling with others or commuting, keep going. But try to spend some time actually reading a book in your hands if you can.) Then post comments about what you've read to social media, or join Goodreads, or find a local book club. Talking about what you've read, and hearing what others think about the same books, can greatly enhance your enjoyment—and allow you to connect with others in some new ways.

# THE JOY OF SEX

The year: 1972. Nixon was running for reelection. NASA had planned the next, and final, Apollo lunar landing. In September, terrorists stunned the world with an attack at the Munich Olympics. And in October, the first copies of *The Joy of Sex* found their way into bookstores and bedrooms across America, including my parents'. I had turned fifteen a few months earlier, so I may not have been the intended audience for the groundbreaking book, but I found myself curious to know what was between its covers.

Sometime around Halloween, I realized I had the house to myself for a couple of hours. I stole into my parents' bedroom like a thief who had already cased the joint, moving directly to my dad's dresser. I opened the top drawer, and underneath the perfectly folded T-shirts I found it: *The Joy of Sex,* by the British physician Alex Comfort. Full of anticipation, I took the book downstairs with me to the living room, where I sat on the wingback chair in front of the fireplace and began to read (and examine the many graphic illustrations).

Well into the evening I sat rapt, turning pages, stopping here, picking up there, losing all track of time—when suddenly I heard the rustle of keys in the front door. I knew it would only be seconds before Mom walked through our little foyer, shouting, "We're home!" I panicked, shoved the book under the chair, and ran upstairs.

As predictable as the grandfather clock's chimes in our house, Mom made her announcement, which was the prompt for me to come down and say hello. I arrived at the threshold of the living room, where nothing was ever out of place, just as Mom's gaze reached the wing chair. "What's that?" she muttered aloud as she crossed the room. She realized it was a book, and, not understanding at first, asked, "How did this get here?" I pretended to be as surprised as she was.

Comfort's positive and affirming perspective on sex and intimacy could not have come at a better time for me. Already, I'd been called out as a "pervert" and "faggot" and even beaten up because some guys in the neighborhood thought I might be gay. My relationship to sex and sexuality was mired in shame and secrecy, but Comfort's book showed me the possibility of a world in which love, intimacy, and sex could be joyful and loving.

*The Joy of Sex* went on to make history, selling more than twelve million copies and spending seventy weeks on *The New*

*York Times* bestseller list. Reviewers noted how Comfort had written "one of the least inhibited books on sex" and one that "is straightforwardly healthy."

Five years later, on a rainy night, with my college roommate away, I first made love to a man, remembering to this day the tenderness of his kiss more than anything else. (Okay, almost anything else!) Bob represented all the passions, possibilities, and precious innocence of my youth. Thank you, Dr. Comfort, for teaching me the lessons I needed to learn about love, intimacy, and sex before I had that first experience.

Then life happened, as it does.

I was on another Bob's deck, with the bright lights of San Francisco behind us and the first wisps of the summer fog creeping in. The attraction was palpable. His finger traced the outline of my nose—and then we kissed. It was our first kiss, romantic and passionate. And even more: it was fraught with the unknown. The year was 1988, still early in the AIDS epidemic, when half of all gay men in the city had been infected with HIV. Bob and I had not yet had the talk ("What is your HIV status?").

There was still so much we didn't know then. A scant two years before, the surgeon general had ruled out "casual" modes of transmission—like mosquito bites, toilet seats, swimming pools, and kissing. But fears lingered, especially with no vaccine or treatment and a frighteningly high death rate. There was also the stigma, and very real consequences: gay men with HIV were ostracized, fired from our jobs, abandoned by our families. Intimacy became woven with fear and shame, kiss by kiss.

By the time Bob and I became bedmates and boyfriends, he'd told me he'd tested positive for HIV (and I had replied that I had not). We engaged in what was first known as "safe sex" but later became called "safer sex," because nothing is absolute. That extra "-er" at the end of the word was a constant reminder that every sexual encounter was potentially perilous and required some degree of vigilance. I remember our anxiety-ridden conversations. "How safe is oral sex?" "What do we do if the condom breaks?" For me, like others in my generation, the plague complicated my coming-out journey: it reinforced notions that homosexuality was "bad," and it bred a firestorm of fear about sex and intimacy that took years (and in my case much therapy) to work through. In large measure, the epidemic erased the joy of sex. Fear of HIV also led me to end my relationship with Bob, a decision I came to regret almost from the moment I made it. (Bob died twenty-seven years later in 2015, not from AIDS or any complications due to HIV, but rather from a rare neuromuscular condition.)

Four years ago I wrote a column for *The Washington Post* about sexual dysfunction, noting that among men in their sixties, about 60 percent acknowledge problems with erections, sex drive, and overall satisfaction. Looking back at that column now, I realize there are two sides to every coin.

I had focused on sexual dysfunction in older people. But as it turns out, many studies report that Americans across just about every demographic group (and not just those of a certain age) are now having less sex than at any other time in at least three decades. Curiously—or perhaps predictably—here we are in the middle of a loneliness epidemic, and we're having less sex than ever. Even more notably, a study published in the *Archives of Sexual Behavior* notes a decline in sexual frequency among Americans of all ages *except*—drumroll, please!—people over seventy. In its most recent year for the annual study, millennials and Gen Xers reported a drop in the frequency with which they have sex, compared with earlier years.

Meanwhile, Baby Boomers and the Greatest Generation say they are having more sex than their age cohort previously reported. That study, like several others, concluded that the quality, not just the quantity, of sex gets better with age.

I also took another wrong turn in that column: I equated sexual satisfaction with frequency—specifically, frequency of orgasm. I should have known better. When I was twenty-six, I had a very fancy-sounding surgery called a retroperitoneal lymph node dissection, a delicate eight-hour procedure to remove more than a dozen cancer nodes from my abdomen. A week or so before the operation, my surgeon talked with me about a common side effect—retrograde, or dry, ejaculation, which means that during orgasm semen flows into the bladder, not out of the penis. "It won't diminish your sexual pleasure," the doctor insisted, although I feared what this potential side effect would mean for me, a guy already struggling with issues around intimacy.

Well, lucky me, I won that lousy side effect lottery and I've not had an ejaculation since. According to the experts at Cleveland Clinic (and my own surgeon), retrograde ejaculation is classified as either a sexual dysfunction or sexual disorder. Both of those mean "abnormal" or "impaired," and for decades—despite having both short- and long-term relationships—that's how I saw myself. Abnormal and impaired. It's really too bad I hadn't kept a copy of *The Joy of Sex* with me to reiterate that when it comes to sex, normal is what you enjoy, hurts no one, and doesn't make you anxious.

Soon after turning sixty, I began to hang out with a fellow tennis player. One evening, Douglas, as I'll call him, told me that he'd had radical prostate cancer surgery, which I knew meant removal of the prostate (and which I wrongly thought meant he could not achieve an erection). "I inject a medication called Caverject into my penis about fifteen minutes before I want to be ready," he explained. "It really works." I'll attest to that, but, more importantly, his openness allowed me to talk about my own performance issues, which didn't seem dysfunctional in that context. In being open about our perceived vulnerabilities, we found connection and comfort—real intimacy.

Hundreds of *Post* readers commented on that essay, helping me to understand how the joy of sex had been misplaced or lost over our lives. A married man wrote that when he and his wife were younger, their goal was to see how many orgasms they could have, and—let me just paraphrase here—they'd had plenty. But then he added, "I think we missed out on a lot of great sex," making a distinction between orgasm and sexual pleasure. "The sex is less frequent now," he continued, "sometimes without erections even after taking a pill, but I am enjoying it more and she certainly is enjoying it more. I think a lot of it has to do with being comfortable with ourselves now, and with each other, and we don't feel like we have to achieve any certain goal. We know that sometimes it's going to flop and that is okay. There are some other times that it is freaking amazing."

A seventy-year-old jumped into the thread here, introducing herself as a woman "with a great sex life and a husband who understands my needs. But have you ever considered that maybe it's the men who are the real problem? Women need a lot more than an erect penis to turn them on. In fact, we don't even need an erect penis to enjoy multiple orgasm." On a roll, she continued, "There's no reason why a man or a woman with some age-related sex problems can't find a way to enjoy physical pleasure without fully reaching orgasm. The journey is more important than the final performance."

In the end, one septuagenarian helped me to come full circle, back to that evening when I first surreptitiously read *The Joy of Sex* as a fifteen-year-old. He wrote: "On reading many of the comments on a limp situation what I find missing is the word INTIMACY. I have been in several long-term partnerships, and what caused them to eventually flounder was the true lack of confidence and intimacy in the relationships. Fortunately for me, now I have been in a close mutual and intimate relationship for almost three decades. A partnership that continually grows and pleasantly surprises both of us. Yes, and it's very pleasantly, arousingly sexual. Without that enjoyment of mutual INTIMACY, there probably would be little sex as one ages."

These days I'd argue we need to have not only more sex but also better sex. The consequences of not doing so are profound. Magdalene Taylor, a writer who explores how desire and digital culture inform identity, argues, "Sex reduces pain, relieves stress, improves sleep, lowers blood pressure and strengthens heart health." She also rightfully points out that "sex is intrinsic to a society built on social connection," which echoes what Comfort, the British physician, wrote more than a half century ago: without love and sex we will remain souls without ties, without connection.

## How to Find More Joy in Sex

Given the number of search results I found when I googled "How can I find more joy in sex?" I'd say a lot of people want to know the answer. As a dauntless journalist, I decided to consult some experts—a handful of escorts (also known as sex workers) who make a living out of delivering happy endings.

In my interviews, I learned a phrase new to me, one that may hold the key to more pleasurable sex and intimacy. Many escorts advertise what's called "the girlfriend experience" or "the boyfriend experience," which speaks to the needs of their clients who want to experience the feeling of intimacy that comes with a committed relationship. Think dates, courting, romance. Research from George Washington University reflects the same trend: one third of men who seek out sex workers are not looking for sex but rather for "emotional intimacy."

One escort (who preferred to remain anonymous) told me that among the top reasons men choose him is companionship. "Vulnerability is built on trust," he explained. "A prolonged text exchange before meeting helps establish some of that, common interests in the bedroom and out, and gauging humor or conversational personality." Similarly, Melissa Petro (no relation), a former escort, writes in *Salon* that she advertised herself and sold what amounted to the girlfriend experience. "This meant that after a man had answered my ad, we'd arrange to meet and have a drink or two, just as if it were a real date."

So, what do these experts advise for people who want to cultivate more joy in their sex lives?

**Be real.** Authenticity is the key to connection, and that requires being honest, even in the most intimate of settings. This includes talking openly about likes and dislikes. Said one escort, "If you're not comfortable talking about these things, try writing them down and sharing that way. Learning how to listen to your partner, whether new or long-term, has the greatest payoff."

**Redefine connection.** "Many people mistake full-on sex as the end-all of achieving a total connection," Matt Stevens, who works primarily in South Florida, told me. "Now more than ever people want to form a human connection, and that can often start as a physical interaction. Many times the ongoing cuddling and kissing with the conversation takes over and intercourse is pushed aside as a human connection is forming. It may actually be preferable to the physical."

**Ask your partner what "good sex" means to them**. As one of my interviewees explained, "Vocabulary matters. Develop yours. And check in with your partner during sex and ask them if they like what's happening if you can't tell. And even if you can tell, still ask, just so they know you're paying attention to the feedback they're giving."

Above all, what I heard is this: there is satisfaction to be had in sex, of course, but the true joy of the experience is the intimacy and connection.

# THE JOY OF AGING

I hope I've earned enough credibility by now that you don't think I'm a name-dropper—because I'm about to do just that. A while back, I had the good fortune to work with Suzanne Somers (as the editorial director of her online program, Sexy Forever, based on her bestselling book of the same name). Over the years, Suzanne has topped the *New York Times* bestseller list with more than fourteen titles, including *A New Way to Age*, *Breakthrough*, and *Ageless*.

We first met—she in her early sixties, me two decades younger—when I made the trip to her Malibu home to kick off our project. Suzanne answered the door herself, shoes off and hair down. Our conversation ranged from funny to serious, but from start to finish she was passionate about one topic: aging.

Suzanne told me she fully expected to live beyond one hundred years. I confessed I wasn't sure I wanted to do that—after all, who wants to be the last one standing? But this was the woman who'd once said: "The biggest myth about aging is that we can't do anything about it. That it's a road to being decrepit, frail, and sick." She was determined to debunk that notion, and by the end of our first meeting, she had me in her camp.

Suzanne lived her life as she wrote about it. She adored her family, she ate organic foods, and she carried a flask of her favorite tequila in her purse. She reveled in telling the world that she and husband, Alan, had sex two (or was it three?) times a day, every day. Despite the stereotype of her as a ditzy blonde, thanks to her role in the sitcom *Three's Company,* Suzanne was formidable and wise, an unstoppable force of life and joy. By personally breaking the mold of what it meant to get older, Suzanne allowed me—and many others—to imagine we might not succumb to becoming decrepit, frail, or sick.

A decade after our first meeting, and long after our online project was behind us, I visited Suzanne and Alan in their Palm Springs house. After ascending to their door in a funicular (think cable car), I joined them for a cocktail (or was it two?), then went on a guided tour of the compound. My favorite stop was what I'd call "the jewelry room," where a large table was covered by her precious and semiprecious gems (organized, natch, by color). Suzanne told a story I'd not heard or read before. Here's how I recall it:

"I believe you can actually program happiness into your mind and body. We're made up of forty trillion cells that communicate with each other nonstop. Every day as I'm waking up I talk to one of those cells. I say, 'I'm healthy! I'm happy! I have love in my life!' I imagine all the cells passing along that message, with all forty trillion of them singing in concert. That visualization keeps me positive and brings me joy!"

"That's what brings you joy—not the jewelry?" I asked, only half-jokingly.

"No, not the jewelry—and no, you can't have a piece of it," she replied, anticipating my very next thought.

By that point I'd already been focused on shifting my perspective when it came to aging, from something frightening, limiting, and dark to a new state of acceptance, confidence, even opportunity. My evolution began as I watched my parents face the inevitable declines in physical health (Dad) and cognitive functioning (Mom), which led me to write *Stupid Things I Won't Do When I Get Old*. In that book I made dozens of pledges about how I planned to age gracefully: Get the hearing aid. Make intergenerational friends. Don't let others render you invisible. Reject any suggestion of disrespect (especially about age). And, most important and the most challenging, stop internalizing everyday ageism, in which we buy into the negative perceptions of what it means to get old in this culture. One example: no longer do I send birthday cards featuring wrinkled old cartoon characters that mock or perpetuate common stereotypes of older people.

I found myself shocked to learn that ageism (the kind we inflict upon ourselves) is associated with earlier death, by as much as seven and a half years according to the World Health Organization, not to mention worsened physical and mental health. You read that right—just thinking and feeling old makes us older than our years. Maybe that's why so many of those inspirational posters remind us that "it's not the length of life, but the depth of life that matters."*

I began to recognize a positive shift in how I viewed myself. I felt more content and confident, less reactive and constrained by preconceived expectations. I also made a deliberate effort to focus on the positive aspects of getting older, happily becoming less of a curmudgeon. Many friends and colleagues also voiced similar sentiments as they crossed the threshold of fifty.

Amy Gorely, who launched a national awareness campaign called Be Bold, Claim Old—a movement to celebrate all ages—frequently speaks about ageism. Now in midlife herself, Gorely told me, "I am so much more comfortable in my own skin, being assured, confident, and leading my own life by my own values, truth, and power as opposed to societal norms. There's been more time for self-reflection, which helps me to be more aware of my strength and challenges." A different friend put it like this: "I no longer care what most people think of me. Well, a lot of the time, anyway. But what I choose to do, I do for myself." To that, I say good is good enough.

Surprisingly, new research corroborates my experience in aging. The authors of a study published in the *Journal of Personality and Social Psychology* note that inner acceptance of aging leads to less

*This quote is widely attributed to Ralph Waldo Emerson, although there's no evidence he ever said or wrote it.

anger and anxiety and greater "calmness and serenity." Similarly, Lawrence R. Samuel, a cultural historian who authors the *Boomers 3.0* blog, argues, "A certain kind of emotional well-being or 'life intelligence' is acquired over the years, perhaps because one simply has greater experience in different kinds of situations and can thus better keep things in perspective." To put things more succinctly, I'd call this wisdom.

Wisdom is, actually, one of the gifts that we're more prone to find in our later years, one that is inextricably linked with joy. A pathbreaking study published in the *Journal of Experimental Psychology* examined the relationship between well-being (a proxy for happiness or joy) and wise reasoning (or wisdom). It turned out that the two scores were correlated—greater wisdom with greater well-being. But much more interesting (at least in this context) is that the older you get, the stronger the correlation. "Wise senior citizens had considerably higher well-being than their unwise peers," note the study's authors. They continue, "With a random sample of Americans, we found that wise reasoning is associated with greater life satisfaction, less negative affect, better social relationships, less depressive rumination, more positive versus negative words used in speech, and greater longevity."

Journalist Maria Shriver has long been a powerful voice when it comes to self-acceptance, especially when it comes to aging. In a recent essay, Shriver describes the many forms of joy that she's experienced as she's gotten older.

> Lately, I've been thinking a lot about aging. I recently turned 66 years old, and while I feel great and I'm grateful to have the gift of my health, I can't help but think of the fragility of time and how fleeting it can be. I never really think of myself as old, but I'm learning that that's a mistake. Recognizing my age allows me to look at things from a different perspective. It helps me see that in fact, the opportunities available to me now are way better than the ones I had when I was in my 20s. It allows me to embrace that while age may just be a number, there is no time to waste. It inspires me to fill my days with people and work that lights me up, keeps me learning, fuels my curiosity, and excites me.

There's an exuberance in the way Shriver embraces and accepts aging that is, frankly, contagious. She also points to the research done by Dan Buettner, who wrote *The Blue Zones*. He professes that maintaining purpose in life can increase your life expectancy by as much as eight years. (Does that mean if we scrap our internal biases *and* seek meaning we can boost our life expectancy by more than fifteen years? I sure hope so.)

Shriver, hardly a slouch in her earlier years as a news reporter, anchor, author, mother of four, and first lady of California, is now "working on things that bring me joy and give me purpose." Those activities include founding the Women's Alzheimer's Movement, creating a media company to produce documentaries and films, and publishing *The Sunday Paper*, a weekly newsletter that reaches millions.

Despite all these résumé accolades, I couldn't overlook that Shriver's Instagram bio leads with none of that, instead focusing on her two most important roles, "Mama & Mama G" (mother and grandmother).

Similarly, in recent years I've come to value my job titles as brother and uncle (or "guncle," which is a gay uncle) over others I've held, like editorial director of a publishing company and national president of a journalism organization. Like many of my friends, my priorities are shifting as I get older. Family is at the top of my list.

I'm aware that none of this could have happened at an earlier stage of my life, despite having had the guidance of Suzanne Somers in my forties. It's taken experiences (often deeply challenging) that have led to some bits of wisdom, none of which I take for granted. I'm reminded of the popular adage: "The meaning of life is to find your gift. The purpose of life is to give it away." That takes time, but more importantly, a willingness to evolve, which only comes with the desire to change. To this point, mythologist Michael Meade writes, "Although an infant becomes a child simply by aging, a person cannot become an elder by simply becoming older. Elders fall into the category of things that are made, not born."

For me, that process of change, and the joy that's come along with it, comes back to a shift in perspective, which is to say how I changed my values and beliefs about aging. Carol S. Dweck, a Stanford psychologist, is best known as the author of *Mindset*. I especially love this passage:

> True self-confidence is "the courage to be open—to welcome change and new ideas regardless of their source." Real self-confidence is not reflected in a title, an expensive suit, a fancy car, or a series of acquisitions. It is reflected in your mindset: your readiness to grow.

And that's how I've come to experience and appreciate the many joys of aging, which are worthy trades for gray hair, face wrinkles, and especially feeling badly about—instead of celebrating—each birthday. While Suzanne Somers didn't live to one hundred—alas, she died in 2023 at age seventy-six—damn if she didn't defy aging every day of her life, and damn if she didn't enjoy the trip.

## How to Embrace Aging

In a column Maria Shriver wrote for *Prevention*, she identifies five concrete steps for banishing a negative mindset about being old. These strategies are culled from dozens of interviews she conducted with people about aging well. They resonate with me and they make a fine road map to navigate those "golden" years.

**Put the kibosh on "anti-aging" anything.** Face and eye creams are just the start—there is a whole industry out there trying to sell products to "prevent" aging. Don't get pulled into that way of thinking. Sure, keep your skin healthy (and beautiful), but don't obsess about some battle you're supposed to be waging.

**Step outside your comfort zone.** It's all too easy to get complacent as we get older, to avoid taking risks and stick with the tried and true. The world can pass you by that way, so don't get mired in old habits and don't be frightened of new things. "I know that saying 'yes' to new things builds confidence, puts me in a beginner's mindset, and enables me to keep learning," Shriver explains.

**Accept that you will experience loss and grief.** It seems that every day I read the obituary of a TV star, rocker, or literary giant who loomed large in my youth. Those hurt, for sure, but not nearly as much as losing a loved one, which is bound to happen more frequently as we get older. "Grief is tough work, but it will teach you that you can survive," Shriver writes.

**Live with purpose.** Too many people spend their lives in unsatisfying careers, looking forward to stopping work at retirement. Then what? Exactly. As Shriver suggests, choose activities that feed your creativity and help you to stay curious and feel engaged and alive. With any luck you'll be too busy to feel cranky.

**Take a moment.** Meditate, go for a walk by yourself, spend some focused time with your children or grandchildren. You'll build greater balance, resilience, and joy. Think. Enjoy. Breathe. Live.

# THE JOY OF UNCERTAINTY

A few months ago, I found myself getting dressed to go out to dinner with a guy I'd met at a dinner party. Choosing what to wear proved a nightmare: button-down shirt or slim-fit pullover, khakis or skinny jeans, loafers or tennis shoes? Finally, I understood the real dilemma at hand: I didn't know if I was going to dinner with a new friend (button-down shirt) or on a first date with a potential beau (skinny jeans). Uncertainty stared back at me from the mirror. I actually found the not knowing both unsettling and exciting, which surprised me, because for most of my life I've hated not knowing how the story ends.

In 2017 I had to face the most insidious uncertainty I could imagine when my sister called to say she'd been diagnosed with ovarian cancer.

The day before Julie called me, our family had been planning a Christmas vacation in Connecticut; the following day, we had no idea where we'd be for Thanksgiving, two weeks later. It was a scary manifestation of one kind of uncertainty—the sudden upending shock, like getting fired, witnessing your house go up in flames, or becoming a crime victim. Without warning, the road ahead—which a moment earlier had been marked with clear mileposts and turnoffs—is no more. Detours, closures, and hazard markers are the new road signs.

At the outset, I couldn't imagine anything worthwhile resulting from our metaphoric detour. But, in the remaining time Julie had with us, I learned not only how to live with uncertainty but to embrace it, which, in turn, allowed me to experience a deeper understanding and love of those close to me.

Random events puncture lives all the time. Sometimes they bring joy—a chance meeting, an unexpected romance, winning the Mega Millions lottery—other times they feel cataclysmic. No matter, they always break up the rhythm of our daily lives.

Certainty can be comforting, for sure, but also a little boring. I'm thinking about some marriages I know, as well as a few friends who've held the same jobs for decades. In my own life, I'm reminded that Julie and I watched just about every Hallmark Channel Christmas movie, knowing that—no matter what—we'd be treated to a happy ending in two hours flat. The commoner will marry the prince, the working girl will snag the widower. The very nature of the rom-com structure provides comfort, but not necessarily joy.

Where's the drama? What about serendipity? How can we learn not to fear the unknown but to embrace it?

I'll admit, for much of my life, I abhorred the unknown because it terrified me. I remember reading Dashiell Hammett's *The Maltese Falcon* in grad school and being deeply unsettled when Charles Flitcraft, a dependable husband and father who thrived on routine, found his life unalterably changed one day. As Hammett wrote, "A beam or something fell eight or ten stories down and smacked the sidewalk alongside him. It brushed pretty close to him, but didn't touch him, though a piece of the sidewalk was chipped off and flew up and hit his cheek. . . . He felt like somebody had taken the lid off life and let him look at the works. . . . He knew then that men died at haphazard like that, and lived only while blind chance spared them."

Back then, my life mirrored Flitcraft's in its routine and ennui. Predictable and safe, with little uncertainty. And then one day, someone took the lid off my life.

It was a completely ordinary April day, in the hours between lunch and dinner, when the doctor sent me down to radiology for a scan. When I returned to his office, he already had the results in his hands: cancer. Two mornings later I woke up after surgery in a hospital bed and wrote in my journal: "None of this was on my personal road map. I suddenly understood that it was all random, and none of it was within my control." My well-ordered life—so appealing in its comfort, predictability, even safety—now seemed precisely the opposite. Even worse, I found myself anxious to fast-forward to the ending of my personal medical thriller. I wanted answers, wanted to see a certain future. Would my hair fall out? (Yes, it did.) Would I survive the cancer? (Well, here I am.)

That's when I noticed an internal shift. When it came to novels, even TV series, I began to realize that I preferred not knowing the final chapter or act. Not only did this allow my imagination to roam, to contemplate different outcomes, but I became more present with the storyline. What if Lily Bart, beautiful and penniless, didn't have to die in Edith Wharton's *The House of Mirth*? What if Derek Shepherd had been taken to a better ER on *Grey's Anatomy*? What if J.R. had died from his gunshot wounds on *Dallas*? I came to appreciate that gasp of surprise, the sheer joy of the plot twist. I started to understand what Eric Kim, a photographer and book author, meant when he wrote, "My joy is precisely NOT knowing what today or the future holds." I appreciated his take on making art, especially that "imprecision, uncertainty of what the final product will look like—this is what makes art so fun!"

Indeed, I found a measure of joy—which only grew over time—in not knowing what today, tomorrow, or the future holds. Possibility. Mind wandering. Yes, uncertainty.

For me, that meant coming to grips with the hard realities of my illness. After I finished eight months of treatment, my psychologist said, "Well, that was like having five years of therapy all at once." What he meant was that while you can learn a lot about yourself in weekly talk sessions, a serious illness provides an unexpected opportunity to go deeper, fast. In my case, I'd hardly been tested in life. I had an overconfidence that manifested in doing thoughtless things (like ghosting a boyfriend or even sneaking into a fancy hotel cocktail party to have a drink or two).

When confronted by the prospect of disfigurement, disability, even death, I lost my sense of invulnerability. Suddenly I had to find an emotional depth I hadn't sought before, a passion for a fight that I didn't want, a consideration for others that was new to me.

And I did. I believe I became a better person. I also came to understand some of the lessons of my illness, much as I did the wisdom of Ralph Waldo Emerson when he wrote, "The years teach much which the days never know." Friends saw the positive changes in me, noting that I appeared more content, even more joyful, despite the challenging circumstances. It may seem counterintuitive, but the sudden uncertainty made me more confident in who I wanted to be.

Early on in Julie's illness, I began talking with my good friend Julia Liss, now a retired professor of history, about uncertainty. Her husband, Greg, had faced a life-threatening illness several years after my cancer diagnosis, so she certainly had a large measure of empathy for my sister and our family. Julia explained that she had initially coped with the uncertainty of her husband's diagnosis by aiming to "master what was going on—understand it, make decisions about treatment, figure out the course to recovery." She relied increasingly on "order as a coping mechanism." When grocery shopping, she told me with a knowing smile, "I'd go down every single aisle, even if I didn't need to. There was the time they reorganized the aisles, and it was chaos!"

When Julia told me about her control-focused strategy, I realized I, too, believed that by maintaining order in my life—attempting to plan out every detail of every day—I could regain control of my sister's life and illness.

Over time, Julia learned that her approach was both exhausting and futile, especially as Greg's condition worsened and his chances of recovery declined. She changed course, telling me, "When things are overwhelmingly hard and scary, and the prognosis is generally not good, sometimes hope lies in the unknown." It took me a few minutes to grasp what she meant as she continued, "Uncertainty and unpredictability—suddenly and surprisingly—are where there's an opening for hope."

It has taken me decades—from my own cancer to Julie's—to realize the truth in the popular aphorism, a heavy paraphrase of Plato's *Apology,* "The only true wisdom is in knowing you know nothing." In between those two malignant milestones, whether it was letting a movie plot or a dinner date unfold on its own or facing any one of life's random twists of fate, I tried to embrace the unknown, appreciate the ride, and find joy in those blurry moments. There is something quite appealing in not knowing until the very end that the butler did it.

Or that, yes, in fact it was a date.

## How to Live with Uncertainty

Are you the kind of person who spends an entire TV show or movie guessing the next plot twist or predicting the ending? Many people approach their own lives that way, striving for certainty and always trying to control their next development as they steer toward a known ending (marriage, a family, a house, a well-paying job . . .). Others watch movies and allow the plot to wash over them, experiencing the twists and turns as they happen, waiting in anticipation to see how it all works out. And they may well live their lives that way as well. Which are you?

If you find yourself struggling with the larger unknowns—the economy, the political landscape, global warfare—you may have a very hard time with uncertainty in everyday life and may find yourself mired in anxiety. Scientists call it "intolerance of uncertainty" and it is highly associated with negative emotions such as fear and worry. (There is even a twenty-seven-point Intolerance of Uncertainty Scale!)

Some of the techniques of cognitive behavioral therapy, what's known as CBT, may be helpful in reining in your anxiety about a situation with a high degree of uncertainty. This kind of therapy can help you deal with overwhelming problems by breaking them down into smaller parts. In the process, you can learn to change negative feelings and patterns to help you feel better. In my experience, CBT gave me techniques to change or rewrite the doomsday video playing in my head. (In case you're wondering, CBT is considered the gold standard psychological treatment, which is to say the best currently available, in effecting positive behavioral change.)

For our purposes, make a list of the uncertainties that bother you, from largest to smallest. Put them all on the list, from war in the Middle East to a friend's bad choice of romantic partner. Then make notes on each:

- Is it even remotely within your control?
- What could you do to affect the outcome?
- What's the worst that could happen? What's the best?
- What effect will the ultimate outcome have on you?

Think about each situation separately and evaluate first your thoughts, then your feelings, about each. Look at the facts and be realistic. Are your thoughts accurate, or distorted? What about how they make you feel, and act? Are those behaviors helpful? How can you use problem-solving skills to navigate one step at a time, instead of jumping ahead in your mind?

These steps won't improve your level of certainty, but they should help you to better direct your energies where they belong and to develop concrete actions you actually control. Try to remember that without uncertainty there would be no serendipity, and who would want to sacrifice that joy?

I also know it won't make a bit of difference in the plot of the next movie you see, either—so why not just sit back and enjoy the show?

# THE JOY OF THE DARK

A few years ago, I decided to head to the "land of fire and ice"—better known as Iceland—in January to attend a yoga retreat at the darkest and coldest time of year. Nearly every one of my friends asked me some version of the same question: "Why don't you wait until summer, when the sun never sets?" To each of them I replied, "I want a chance to see the magic of the aurora borealis, which can only be viewed with darkness as its backdrop." I also hoped there might be lessons to be found in the long, dark days of Iceland's winter that could help guide me through the seemingly endless midnight of my grief and loss. After all, there's a reason Galileo named the northern lights after Aurora, the Roman goddess of dawn. If ever a soul needed a new day, I did.

As I revealed to the fourteen complete strangers in our first-night welcome circle: "I've been living in a dark hole for the past two years. Not in an ice cave or anything like that, but the recent suicide of a friend added to a series of painful losses, including the death of my parents, punctuated by my husband's exit from our marriage in between Mom's and Dad's passing. I'm looking for a new beginning."

I found myself in good company with my fellow travelers, most of whom were also seeking new chapters—after a divorce, job loss, or early retirement; recovering from an illness; grieving the death of a loved one; or seeking a new path for midlife (one with greater meaning than jobs with fancy titles, enviable salaries, and the attendant creature comforts).

My choice of a winter travel date had been based on science, not whimsy. Had I not become a writer, I'm sure I'd have chosen to be a meteorologist, which is to say I grew up as a nerd—specifically, a weather geek. For my thirteenth birthday, I asked my parents for a rain gauge, a recording barometer, and an anemometer (a device that measures wind speed and direction). With my new gear I became an actual reporting station for the weather service, calling in daily. I attended New York City's Stuyvesant High School, known for its advanced science and math curriculum, although I stuck with English and French classes as much as I could. I did, however, manage to do the required frog dissection in tenth grade. Bravo to me!

I left Stuy, as we called it, well trained in the scientific method, "The approach that science uses to gain knowledge, based on making observations, formulating laws and theories, and testing theories or hypotheses by experimentation," according to *Oxford Reference*. Put another way: I believed every problem had a solution if you only studied the data.

When I tried to determine my best odds of seeing the northern lights, the data seemed unequivocal: visit in the dead of winter, during a dark and moonless week, then target an area known for minimal cloud cover, what the locals refer to as "lágmarks skýjavík." To help me, I downloaded a five-star-rated app called My Aurora Forecast, which promised "you'll be seeing the Northern Lights in no time." I chose a set of retreat dates that would take me to the same location, during the same week of the year, when the aurora had previously made itself—or herself—visible.

Sure, I'd done my homework, but I also knew that the northern lights are not like Old Faithful. They are notoriously unpredictable; they don't run on a schedule. One travel website warned: "The Northern Lights are Mother Nature's creation and as such we can't even use historical data to predict how likely you are to witness a display."

I also knew many people, including a niece and her then boyfriend, who had come away from their Icelandic trips disappointed. After all, apps cannot take into account the frequency and intensity of sun activity or the solar winds, nor can meteorologists accurately forecast cloud cover. Science may be able to predict, but it can't guarantee a sighting of the lights.

On day one in Reykjavík, I could tell my odds of witnessing the lights in the capital city were slim at best. I didn't need an app to tell me that—just my eyes. Blazing café windows brightened dark mornings and evenings, and many roofs remained illuminated throughout the night, bringing "daylight" to the dark sky. In addition to all this light pollution, a dense cloud cover obscured the skies. (That isn't to say the aurora is *never* visible in Reykjavík. It is—but it's about as common as seeing the singer Björk sitting in your hotel lobby.)

By the middle of the week, eager to improve our odds, my fellow pilgrims and I boarded an Air Iceland Connect commuter flight to make the forty-minute journey to Akureyri, a small town north of the Arctic Circle. We then caravanned to a remote ski lodge, known as Klængshóll Lodge, home to Icelandic ponies and surrounded by pristine waterfalls and miles and miles of virgin snowfields. No cafés out there. No lights anywhere, in fact.

We were now in the auroral zone, or what's known as the Oval. High in the sky above the geomagnetic North Pole, this is where the elusive aurora is most likely to manifest itself. Our lodge, once a sheep farm, promised on its website to be "the perfect place to witness this natural phenomenon."

The sun fell below the horizon by three thirty every afternoon, with darkness overtaking us soon after. That first night, with partly cloudy skies and frigid temperatures, my aurora app registered only a 30 percent chance of experiencing the northern lights. No matter, our entire group—including me—believed *that* night would be *the* night.

We stayed up. We saw nothing. I knew deep down that a five-star app, a spot-on location, and the strongest of beliefs couldn't blow clouds out of the sky or fire up a solar shower. Still, we hoped to experience this joy—and oddly enough, that hope was a joy in itself.

In recent times, I've come to understand what's called "anticipatory grief," especially as it relates to my sister's illness. But I hadn't known about "anticipatory joy." Alex Lickerman, a physician who is the former director of primary care at the University of Chicago (and a practicing Buddhist), has described it as commonly being greater than the joy brought to us by the thing we're looking forward to. "This is often because what we expect an experience to be like is often not what it's like and the difference between our expectations and reality mutes our experiential joy," he writes in *Psychology Today*. "But it's also because anticipating a pleasure is itself intrinsically pleasurable."

Anticipatory pleasure is so important to his sense of well-being, Lickerman's written, that he now plans his life in such a way as to try to have something to look forward to. "This can be finishing an interesting blog post, working on my next book, going to a movie or a play with my wife, playing with my son, reading a good book, getting errands done, or even organizing my desk. I've learned the activity needn't be large or significant or meaningful—just something I look forward to, even a little bit."

My literary agent, Richard Pine, has long been a proselytizer of this same strategy, always making sure he has two fun things to look forward to on his calendar (one of which is a scuba diving adventure with friends). I've followed his lead and currently have planned a pizza party at my house in a few weeks and a long summer weekend with friends at my cabin in the Blue Ridge

Mountains. What's especially appealing about anticipatory joy is that we can experience it even when we're depressed or sad, writes Lickerman. "Our brains are so constituted that we're able to feel more than one thing at a time—even diametrically opposed feelings."

We saw nothing that first night at the lodge. The following morning, after a vigorous yoga session and a hearty breakfast, I happened upon this somewhat obscure if not mystical blog entry written by a local: "No matter how hard you try, you cannot get rid of darkness. . . . In order to [erase] darkness, you must do something with light, because the light is the only thing that actually exists."

There is always darkness in the space that surrounds our planet. But we find light when we face the sun. As the director Stanley Kubrick once put it, "However vast the darkness, we must supply our own light." I suddenly understood that before I could see my path illuminated, I'd first need to seek out the light within me.

Looking back over that week, I could see that light had revealed itself in unexpected places, as a new spirit of playfulness permeated our group. On a glacier hike, wet and freezing from blinding snow and sleet, two of our group marched onto the slippery ice and spontaneously assumed a one-legged pose that made the rest of us laugh.

On a snowshoeing trek, my new friend Tracy took a tumble; she wasn't hurt, but she couldn't get up. She started to laugh, and then even cackle, which proved infectious. With each passing day I found myself smiling more—even laughing out loud—which researchers say can decrease stress hormones and increase immune cells and infection-fighting antibodies, promoting an overall sense of well-being. Joy!

Light, I came to understand during my time in Iceland, is not only measured by watts and lumens, but also smiles and laughter, made even brighter in sharing with others. I believe the same argument can be made for joy.

By our second-to-last evening, with temperatures way below zero Celsius, I had given up on seeing the goddess of dawn. The app and the weather forecast had promised us light; both had let us down repeatedly. After dinner, the hours ticked by. I finally turned in close to midnight, sliding under the heavy down comforter in resignation.

Forty minutes later I heard a voice shout, "Get up!" Then another, "Get out!" I pulled on my clothes—and a flimsy cotton bathrobe—and ran out into the frigid night to behold a neon-green light show rising into the dark sky from behind the mountains. There she was, the aurora borealis. Dawn at midnight. Light in the darkness.

Within moments, the northern lights were in full flight—turned up to maximum wattage—dancing wildly across the darkness. Driven by the powerful solar winds, they dashed left and then right, undulating, speaking a proprietary language of their own. Magical and mystical, just as reported. Soon our entire group, outside in the bitter cold, found itself cast in the light of the night. To my utter surprise—and delight—I imagined my late mother,

her free spirit stitched into the dancing lights, speaking to me from the heavens.

Soon after that otherworldly experience, alas, the retreat came to an end. I'd made new friends, learned new poses, and witnessed the northern lights. I knew that my planning, my rational and scientific approach, had laid the groundwork for this viewing. But I also understood that my laser focus on finding light on the outside, on seeing Aurora, had nearly blinded me to the other lights in my midst. There was so much of it in my new friends, my fellow travelers—and, to my surprise, even in myself. I couldn't escape the fact that it was only after I'd let go of my expectations and the scientific method that I witnessed the joy of the dancing green light show in the nighttime sky.

Two days later, on my flight back to the United States from Reykjavík, I thought about a passage from Viktor Frankl's book *Man's Search for Meaning*, which chronicles his experiences as a prisoner in the Nazi concentration camps during World War II. He imagines he's speaking with his wife, "struggling to find the *reason* for my sufferings, my slow dying."

> I sensed my spirit piercing through the enveloping gloom. I felt it transcend that hopeless, meaningless world, and

> from somewhere I heard a victorious "Yes" in answer to my question of the existence of an ultimate purpose. At that moment a light was lit in a distant farmhouse, which stood on the horizon as if painted there, in the midst of the miserable grey of a dawning morning in Bavaria. "Et lux in tenebris lucet"—and the light shineth in the darkness.

My return trip ended at my front door at close to two a.m., more than eighteen hours after leaving Iceland. Stepping out of the Uber, I instinctively looked up into the night sky, seeking Aurora (or maybe Mom—I wasn't sure). I snapped a photo with my iPhone and was astounded to see an eerie greenish glow in the sky. I laughed at myself, because I realized I'd traveled all those miles, made all those calculations in search of that magical light, and here it had been with and within me all along. The only difference: now I had the capacity to see it.

## Making the Most of Anticipation

It's all too easy to get locked into the dread of what's in store—a doctor's appointment, a tough meeting, even a family get-together—but don't miss out on the run-up to something pleasurable as a way of extending the good feelings around it. The "anticipatory joy" you feel in advance of a fun or pleasurable experience heightens it, so make the most of it.

Challenge yourself to finding something every day that you're looking forward to. It could be something small and not too far off (playing a game later that day, visiting friends over the weekend), or larger and further in the future (planning a big vacation next year, looking forward to a family member's birthday—or your own). It could be your favorite dinner (mine is roast chicken with new potatoes and grilled asparagus) at the end of a long day. The point is to think about it, savor the anticipation, and allow the enjoyment to permeate the day.

As you know by now, I always find it helpful to write things down to make them real. I have a small chalkboard in my kitchen with the top three things I'm most looking forward to. I check it daily, erasing pleasures that have come, and adding new ones as I think about them. Worried you won't have anything to look forward to? I promise if you focus on it you do. Joy is always there; we just need to open our eyes and hearts.

# THE JOY OF JULIE

When I stood up at my sister's memorial service to give one of her eulogies, I introduced myself as "Julie's brother." I explained that of all the roles and identities I've had in my life, both personal and professional, none gave me greater pleasure or meant more to me.

From the day my baby sister came home in April 1962, that blond tyke upended our family. She was a force, a ham, and she soon earned a nickname—Instigator—that stayed with her for the rest of her life. My sister's friends remembered her as "tough," "a fighter," a girl who stood up to others. Her lifelong friend Diane reminded me, "Julie had a mind of her own. She wasn't afraid to say what she thought but she was always kind." These traits stayed with her until the end. Oh, Julie did have one other defining characteristic—her big toothy smile—reflecting the joy within.

# THE JOY OF JULIE

My earnest search for joy began the year Julie learned she had this awful cancer. It wasn't a conscious decision, but one born of necessity. How could I deal with her suffering? How could I prepare to let her go, if and when the time came? I had to find some crumb of joy, if only to make it through two-thousand-plus days. To paraphrase the thirteenth-century philosopher Thomas Aquinas: "Man cannot live without joy."

I started researching this book during Julie's illness, and I relied on much of what I learned to help me get through the darkest days. Or was it the other way around? Did my experiences during those five-plus years become part of the research, allowing me to understand the many dimensions of joy and suffering? I'm not sure. Yet.

I think about how Julie helped me to recognize joy. Right now, I'm focusing on memory—our ability to reach back to happy and not-so-happy times—to unearth those shards of joy. I remember the evening I came out to Julie, when we were both still teens, anxiety garbling my words. Finally, I delivered the punch line, "I am gay." Immediately, Julie began laughing uncontrollably, what I thought bordered on hysterical. Then she delivered her own one-two, "Well, I'm a lesbian." Now, it was my turn to be shocked, aghast. "Oh my god, my baby sister is a dyke," I told my closest friend a few days later. "I've never met a lesbian before." From that time on, Julie and I had a special bond, and just writing this paragraph brings a big, familiar smile to my face.

Throughout our lives, Julie and I wrote each other letters—yes, real pen-on-paper missives, starting when I went off to camp in the early '70s. I saved most of them, including the letter that had three Valium tabs affixed with Scotch tape to the ruled paper—a yellow (2 mg), a blue (5 mg), and a pink (10 mg)—"to be used in case of emergency." A few years later, another letter shows how we had changed roles; she'd become my protector, writing with surprising wisdom for a twenty-one-year-old.

> I hope you have decided to end your second adolescent drug period. It worries me when you tell me that you're snorting heroin and tripping. And if you must do this bullshit—at least do it when you're in a better emotional mood. . . . Anyway, all I want to say is I love you very, very, very much and I want you to be careful. Remember what Grandma always says: "Everything in moderation." Love, Julie

Each of these letters and postcards is in her signature handwriting, evidencing her enthusiasm with loopy capital letters and a surfeit of exclamation points! As I sit here at my desk, Julie's letters are in piles around me, grouped by decade. Each one is an old friend; each one chokes me with its own specific memory; each one makes my heart sing. She seems alive on paper, the joy of her handwriting connecting us, both then and now.

It's hard to skip over the darkness and the lessons her illness brought to our family. A few days before Julie died, her daughter Jessie wrote a letter to her future self, from the "before Mama died" Jess to the "after Mama died" version of herself.

> Yesterday, your mama decided that she will die on Friday. Friday, June 30th. She decided to die in four days. And so you entered liminality. The space between decision and action. Between deciding to die and dying. Four days has since shrunk to three. I write to you with three days left to remind you that your mama is beautiful and brave. That she is skinny as hell and she sleeps fifteen hours a day and when she shifts positions in her bed she shouts with a shot of fresh pain. She is the bravest person you've ever known. Be brave now too, like your mama.

As the end approached, I observed—in awe—how Julie's innate traits, her essence, helped to guide her through the decision of choosing to end her life through what's called medical aid in dying. Simply put, MAID, as it's referred to, allows a person with a terminal illness to take control of how and when they die.

Again, Jess wrote on her blog: "It has been five years of pain and fear and love so bright it is blinding."

I've read and reread this sentence over many times, and each time I am surprised, actually overwhelmed, by the allusion to a "love so bright it is blinding." Light, not dark. Bright, not gloomy. Love, not loss. This was our Julie.

Three months before her death, Julie asked for a birthday party. "Of course!" we told her. Although sixty-one is not a traditional milestone birthday, Julie had taught us that each and every year alive is to be celebrated. We hadn't expected to be here; we hadn't expected *her* to be with us. For my sister, this birthday was more miracle than milestone. I struggle in trying to translate feelings into words. At a time when so many, including myself, would understandably be sad or depressed, even angry (not that she wasn't from time to time), Julie wanted to honor—and celebrate—all that she had in her life. She was grateful for so much. We were, too.

Oh, yes, we would plan a blowout birthday party for her.

Four days before the celebration, we gathered around our separate laptops for Julie's quarterly oncology checkup via Zoom. As soon as her oncologist, Jason Konner, logged on, I knew from his expression that we were getting bad news. He was gentle but direct with my sister: she had exhausted all legitimate treatment options. My sister took in his assessment and said to us, "As best I can, I want to enjoy the time I have left."

Then, after just a beat or two, Julie smiled awkwardly, launching into an off-key (okay, it was awful) rendition of Carol Burnett's end-of-show song, "I'm So Glad We Had This Time Together." Once done with the refrain, Julie tugged her earlobe as if to say goodbye—just as we'd seen Burnett do countless times throughout our childhood. As I clicked on the "Leave Meeting" button, I could still see Julie's big smile in the little Zoom box. She'd found equanimity, which is about maintaining an inner calm and steadiness regardless of what's happening in your life. One of the most elusive emotional states, equanimity may also be one of the deepest sources of joy.

Our planned celebration quickly morphed into a combined birthday bash and—what should I call it?—going-away party. We knew it had to be especially festive in spite of the sobering prognosis. "We'll have games!" exclaimed one of my nieces. Val, one of Julie's closest friends, had spent a week feverishly fashioning a piñata, with interior wooden supports covered by layers of papier-mâché, painted in teal (the official color of ovarian cancer advocates). The stenciled lettering read "Beat the Sh*t Out of Cancer." Frankly, it was a sight to behold—and to destroy.

Joy and sorrow, celebration and grief. I wondered: How do we simultaneously hold such diametrically opposed emotions? In *The Book of Joy*, the Dalai Lama and Archbishop Desmond Tutu talk much about these contradictory duads, making the case that it's possible for us to be joyful in the face of our daily struggles—everything from a flat tire or job loss to a marriage that breaks down or even serious illness and death. Tutu observed, even as he was suffering from prostate cancer, "We are fragile creatures, and it is from this weakness, not despite it, that we discover the possibility of true joy." I noted that Tutu used the phrase "true joy," which I can only imagine is the purest or most heightened form, just as sorrow and grief are the most acute manifestations of loss.

If I understand the archbishop correctly, these challenges crack us open, creating pain—sometimes wrenching pain—but it is in this opening that we connect with our essence, and the hearts of others, realizing the joy that always lives in our midst. Not as lauded as Archbishop Tutu or the Dalai Lama, but no less wise, my dear friend Jen Perciballi, whose older brother, Steve, died at age fifty-two a few years ago, wrote me soon after Julie's death, "Love is our most wonderful human emotion, and it comes at the price of grief. That is the trade-off and part of our human experience. But boy does the grief suck."

Julie took the first whack at the piñata, cracking the outer casing, her well-defined triceps reminding me of her as a lanky teen, with her always-on smile, when she played competitive softball. We clapped. We hooted. We hollered. We each got our turn with the plastic bat, laughing uproariously as we released years of rage and pain. Whack! Whack! Whack! Finally the globe burst open, littering the deck with KitKats, gummies, pansy seed packets, and other goodies.

Next up were the speeches, always the heart and soul of our parties. But what to say at your sister's last birthday? I didn't know. All I understood was that this party was a gift to us—a way to celebrate the day, to celebrate her life. Later, Julie would tell me, quite pleased, "It was like my memorial service, except that I got to hear everything." I replied, trying to dredge up a bit of my usual humor, "People seem to like you, too."

Our brother, Jay, held up an oversize portrait of Julie he'd painted when she was sixteen. Her big, goofy smile at the party was the same as in the painting, as was the devilish—Instigator!—twinkle in her eyes. The tawny-blond hair in the portrait was now a silvery gray, but the spark of life, of her joy, was unchanged. Jay said to all of us: "Her spirit, her energy, I've never met anyone like her. She just throws her energy out there and then she gets it back. Just an amazing person. Julie's handled her illness with so much grace and strength." Then Jay turned to Julie, held her, and said, "I love you." I took note of Jay's inclusion of Newton's third law: for every action in nature there is an equal and opposite reaction. Julie emanated serenity and delight, curiosity and generosity, and most of all gratitude. We could all see the joy on her face.

When my turn came, I uncharacteristically chose to forgo words. Instead I asked everyone to hold hands and to focus their love directly on my sister. I struggled out loud with my confusion about holding conflicting emotions at the same time. I looked around at our friends and family and saw tears and heard sobs. But I also noted the reverberation of laughter, of surprise, of delight—the whispers of joy—at being together one last time. "How lucky are we?" I said to those closest to me as we moved on to the two chocolate birthday cakes, one symbolizing celebration, the other loss.

I can only describe the entire afternoon as positively otherworldly. As my niece Jessie wrote later, "She is herself in life and in death. Full of vitality. Full of song." We were inhabiting that liminal space between life and death, a space large enough to hold both our joy and our sorrow.

How odd to feel anything remotely like joy at such a dark juncture. "Odd" is not the right word. Mind-blowing. Weird. F***ing weird. Always the ruminator—if not the troublemaker—I thought back to how we'd experienced joy since Julie's diagnosis nearly six years earlier. Of course, I now had the benefit of an expanded understanding of how joy manifests.

I thought about the recent August when our family rented a beach house in Rhode Island, a shingled cottage reminiscent of the house where we'd spent childhood summers. I traveled from North Carolina, Julie and her family from New Jersey, and Jay and his family from Connecticut. After our vacation, which included competitive canoeing, daily cook-offs, and a raucous game of hearts (in which my sister was definitely peeking at Jay's cards), Julie sent us an email.

> I sat at the house one night with you all there and imagined the scene with me just faded from the landscape. It was actually a comforting feeling knowing that I either was going to stay a part of this scene for real or be remembered in stolen thoughts and pangs of sweet remembrance and ribbing (hopefully)! Like, if Julie was here she would be "shooting the moon" (ha!). From time to time I feel as though I'm living between the immortal and real worlds. It definitely lets me enjoy the moments with my favorite people (like you all 🙂) on weeks such as this one! And the longer away from the last or next CT scan the better!

My sister-in-law Nancy wrote back:

> So often, we humans try to avoid or deny challenging topics—as if they might disappear! I have found in my "limited experience" that embracing and exploring our fears enables us to be open and vulnerable and can lead to deeper connection to others, especially our loved ones, if we allow it. I hope you know whether you're in the room or not, you bring a smile to my face and heart. You are joyous (maybe too much so, sometimes, haha) and that is your gift, today and forever.

In the midst of Julie's illness, I interviewed Charles Mathewes, a professor of religious studies at the University of Virginia, and a contributor to *Joy and Human Flourishing*. I asked him about the mystery I felt about experiencing joy and sorrow simultaneously. He assuaged my fears, telling me that joy is not only an experience that might leave you "particularly giddy," but that "it renders the world more vivid, more vibrant to you. . . . I think of joy as an experience where, in some ways the bottom drops out or maybe the ceiling lifts off and you see an amplitude of reality." Mathewes elaborated. "Joy can be amplified in the moment when there are other people who are experiencing the same thing as you, or are willing to experience the same thing as you, or are seeking to experience the same thing as you. It's the reverberating—or communal—responses with other people that can make such a difference and can help us experience joy at a time where we might ordinarily think there's none."

We like our stories to end on a happy note, but as you already know, this one does not. Julie died in the shank of the afternoon on June 30, 2023, surrounded by our family and her dog, Scruffy. That morning we held our Julie, hugged her, and laughed together as my sister, with her smile undiminished, waved goodbye, no doubt meaning to allow us some measure of peace, holding at bay the sorrow and grief consuming us.

These days I again find myself thinking about what Angela Williams Gorrell wrote in *The Gravity of Joy*: "[Joy] has grit, it isn't fluffy or ephemeral. Joy is what we feel in our bones when we feel connected to what is good, beautiful, meaningful." Or, as Julie's best friend, Jenny, relayed to us at the memorial service: "To say that Julie sucked the marrow out of life is an understatement. Never bored. Never idle. Always grateful."

That is the joy of Julie.

# EPILOGUE

When I look in the mirror these days, usually while shaving, I appear to be the same person I was a few years ago. Same haircut. Same button-down shirts. Same blue eyes. But I know I'm not the same. What I experienced during Julie's illness (2,075 days from diagnosis to death) changed me in ways I don't fully understand—yet, or perhaps ever. At times it's as though I'm a stranger to myself. It's as though I took a long, life-changing journey, and now I'm back home. The house looks the same, but it's not. How do I make sense of these past years?

I started this book wondering what business I had writing about how to find joy in daily life, even during hard times. I had plenty of reasons—death, divorce, illness—to think I was not only the wrong person, but that I didn't even deserve joy. Yet something happened to me in the past handful of years. Something good. Something profound. Something unexpected, given the frequency and volume of loss and grief I had experienced. I found joy.

I found joy in the everyday.

I found even more joy when I sought it out.

I found the greatest joy of all when I looked within.

One of the first things I came to understand was that I had to find a way to settle into myself. I had been off-kilter for so long, so disconnected from everything. I needed to find equanimity after losing my balance, to reconnect with myself after a long period of disconnection and fracture. I needed to resolve that dissonance between the familiar face in the mirror and the new feelings I had within.

I still feel it most keenly when I look in that mirror. *Who is that?* I'll wonder. It's not the emergence of eye bags, or mouth wrinkles, or fissures in my brow that give me pause; I have learned to accept these gratefully as my reward for longevity. I am happy to be here, after all. What feels "off" is the distance between what I see in my eyes, which is a dullness, even a vacancy, and what I feel in my heart, which is a surprising joy. I've examined myself repeatedly, trying to weave two mes into one (all the while attempting to shave without nicking myself).

The grief that has dulled my eyes is undeniable, but I see I've begun to create space for joy within me, and hold it. I did that through all the many things I've talked about in this book—everything from keeping a gratitude journal ("I'm grateful for chocolate ice cream") to embracing my suck (thank you, tennis). Yes, you have to feel, even the really hard stuff—*especially* the hard stuff—to find the road to joy. As Julie's oncologist Jason Konner told me, we must "open the heart and soul to profound feelings and connections." Even the deep and dark feelings. Those most of all, I think.

Yes, sometimes closing up and disengaging seems so much easier. As Konner cautioned me, "Disengagement is a protective mechanism employed, consciously or not, to avoid the pain." But engagement has its advantages, as I've begun to learn. And in that engagement is the seed of joy.

A few years ago, I spent nearly a week in Thailand, speaking at a United Nations–sponsored conference on aging. Once the confab had wrapped up, I flew to the northern province of Chiang Mai, home to myriad craft shops, dozens of Buddhist temples, and several elephant preserves.

I visited one of those refuges, the Elephant Nature Park, about two hours north of the city. As we tourists climbed out of the buses, we were directed to change out of our street clothes into a uniform that made no distinction between women and men, young and old, trim and thick. I donned the blousy pants that resembled culottes and an oversize shirt adorned with a rainbow of elephants that could rival any ugly Christmas sweater. I looked, as did my fellow tourists, ridiculous.

No matter, the elephants rejoiced to see us despite our sartorial silliness, eagerly eating out of our hands and allowing us to touch them—even rub them lightly. I asked one of my fellow travelers to snap a few photos of me among the elephants. "No one would believe this outfit," I said to myself, forgetting for a moment that I wasn't the main attraction. Just as he began to take pictures, I reached out with my right hand, toward the elephant's massive trunk, to pet it as though it were a dog's snout. I expected it to be anything other than what I felt, but . . . surprise! That trunk—so rough and gnarly—sandpapered my hand and sent shivers up my spine. Egads. And then snap, snap, snap, the moment was captured. I've never seen my mouth so open, so wide. Was this pure terror or pure joy? I couldn't tell—but I could see that it was pure!

When I posted the photo on Facebook, I did so with the self-deprecating comment, "With this photo I'll never get a boyfriend." But despite a few snarky responses, the overwhelming majority of replies began to help me to see that picture, and myself, differently. As I read through the comments, I had to acknowledge that my essence, the kernel of who I am, seemed visible—to me, to my friends, to just about everyone—for the first time since I was a kid with a double cowlick and an easeful smile.

Here are just a few things my friends wrote:

> "I'd say you'd get exactly the RIGHT boyfriend 🙂"
>
> "This just screams JOY!"
>
> "This is such a fabulous photo. . . . Glad you're having so much fun."
>
> "I love the outfit and the enthusiasm!"

"Who cares about a boyfriend when YOU'RE WEARING AN ELEPHANT SHIRT & PETTING AN ELEPHANT AT THE SAME TIME!!!! 😜🤗😎"

Looking at the photo now, I see my glee, delight, and awe. Yes, this is the face of joy. I've now come to believe that joy is at the core of all of us, but as we grow up, it's hidden, overshadowed, even distorted. But not erased.

That photo is now one of my favorites, reminding me of the value of pure and honest expression, the importance of letting your silly flag fly, and the ease of simply being real or authentic. It's still not entirely in my nature to love myself as much as I love this photograph, but I'm trying.

As I write this it's the winter solstice, the shortest, darkest day of the year. Julie died six months ago. I have just returned from the Farmers' Market Pavilion, where a crowd gathered for our town's annual Solstice Lantern Walk. As twilight turned to dusk and then to darkness, the stars began their nocturnal dance and the parade of illuminated floats—a giant crescent moon, a dragon, an owl—along with a paper menagerie of butterflies, dolphins, deer, and a gaggle of snow geese, were dispatched along with their human puppeteers on what's known as Riverwalk.

My friend and neighbor, Bridget Booher, described the gathering in a magazine story a few years ago: "Couples holding hands and teenagers in packs. Babies in strollers and elderly in wheelchairs.

Some people walked over together from nearby homes while others drove in from hours away." Bridget took note of a cluster of young people who sported glowing lightsabers; I was riveted by a giant egret—an oversize puppet on stilts—that bowed down to passersby. Everywhere, as my friend reported, "there were bursts of laughter and exclamations of wonder."

That night I walked with nearly 1,500 friends, neighbors, and strangers. I was side by side with two dear friends, all of us suffering in different ways. I felt a real sense of belonging to something bigger than myself, than ourselves. All together creating light in the darkness; all together making joy out of the dark. "This is the joy you make," I said to myself.

~

I don't want to end this book. To do so is to close a chapter, to turn a corner, to move ahead—to say, finally, that my sister is gone and I am still here. Still, I know it's time.

Wait! Wait! One more story. The night before Julie died, our family slept as one organism under one roof. From the basement couch, I texted Julie and Jay on the floors above:

STEVEN: Good night, sibs

JAY: Good night 😘

JULIE: Good night to the best big brothers in the whole world 💛💛💛

JAY: Love you to the moon and back!!

STEVEN: And to the bestest sister ever ❤❤❤

Thank you for joining me on this journey. I hope that you, too, will find joy, and share it with others as I have tried to do here.

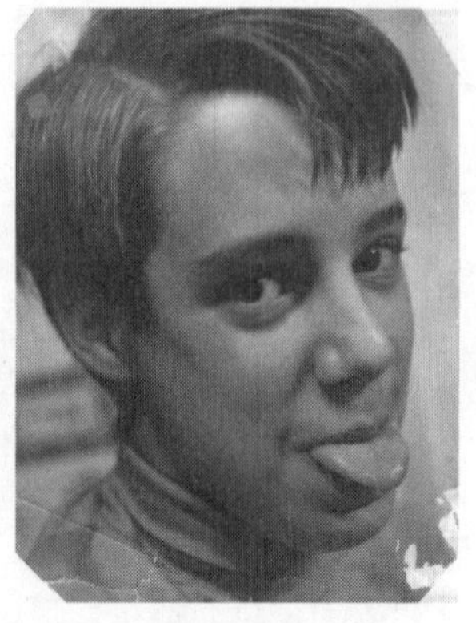

For many years I taped this photograph, an outtake from less silly ones, on the bathroom mirror to remind myself of the joy within.

*Photo credit: The Petrow Family*

Is this pure terror or pure joy? I couldn't tell—but I could see that it was pure! Later, I came to see that this photo revealed my long-hidden essence.

*Photo credit: A fellow traveler to the elephant refuge in Chiang Mai, Thailand, 2019*

Whoops! Surfing has long been one of my greatest joys. In this photo I'm wiping out but exhilarated—the perfect example of "embrace your suck."

*Photo credit: The Petrow Family*

Jay (left), Julie, and me in our Wonder Bread years. Southampton, Long Island, circa 1966. For the rest of our lives we posed for photographs with our little sister between Jay and me. There's an empty space in our hearts now, but these kinds of memories of joy help me to remember the love.

*Photo credit: The Petrow Family*

At our parents' house in Southampton, September 2022. I remember this day so vividly because of the beach walk Julie and I took that day. That evening, she asked me to write a draft of her obituary. No matter, my sister's smile was always there.

*Photo credit: Frankie Alduino*

# ACKNOWLEDGMENTS

I am a lucky fellow to have had two inspirational New York City public school English teachers, Marcia Lippman and the late Charles Neumeier. Each inspired in me a love of reading and writing, with their impact reminding me of what Albert Einstein once said: "It is the supreme art of the teacher to awaken joy in creative expression and knowledge." I thank them both for what they awoke in me.

Maria Shriver has been a teacher of a different kind. Decades later, and many miles from New York, I received an unexpected boost that taught me how serendipity can be an amazing friend. In early 2022, my literary agent received an email from Maria, who had read a column of mine in *The Washington Post* about seeking joy in difficult times. "Do you think Steven would be interested in writing a book about this topic?" Umm, yes. As it turns out, this assignment provided me with a lifeline during one of the most challenging times I've known. Not surprisingly, I'm often asked what it's like to work with Maria. "Not only is she smart, but she thinks big," I reply. "She's also wise and kind, vulnerable and authentic." Thank you, Maria, for all that, and for all that you do.

I'm also grateful to the entire team at Penguin Random House: Isabelle Alexander, Diandra Alvarado, Lynn Buckley, Chantal Canales, Meighan Cavanaugh, Tricia Conley, Julie Faulkner, Megan Gerrity, Bridget Gilleran, Olga Grlic, Lavina Lee, Meg Leder, Shelby Meizlik, Nick Michal, Caitlin Morgan, Lauren Morgan Whitticom, Jason Ramirez, Kate Stark, Mary Stone, and Brian Tart. I am deeply thankful to my editor, Amy Sun, who helped guide and shape this book (and me in the process). All writers should be so fortunate.

At Shriver Media, including the Open Field imprint and *The Sunday Paper,* Meghan Rabbitt, Lauren Westphal, and Jaclyn Levin have welcomed me into the fold.

By now, I've lost track of how many books Richard Pine at InkWell Management has represented for me. I'm always deeply appreciative of his keen editorial sense, his unflagging support, and—in recent years—an even deeper friendship. At InkWell, Kim Witherspoon, Michael Carlisle, Gideon Pine, and Eliza Rothstein also have my thanks. Best literary agency ever!

At *The Washington Post,* Pooh Shapiro remains a constant friend, a great editor, and a joy to work with. Ditto for my now lifelong colleague and friend, *Post* reporter Lena Sun. I'll start and end with "thank you."

I don't know what to say about Roseann Foley Henry. She is my right hand. And my left one. If I had a third hand, she would be that, too. She is funny and she is wise. RH, my nickname for her, has been by my side for more than a decade as my "inside" editor; she knows my life and my voice almost better than I do, and improves everything I write.

Ross von Metzke is my Left Coast hand. For more than ten years he's been my social media guru—posting, commenting, and tweeting as me, even when I'm onstage or asleep. He knows the subtleties of my opinions and has my credit card number.

Early on in the life of this book, I benefited from the assistance of two Duke students, Darcy Blaylock and Caroline Sullivan, who became my prized researchers, each doing massive digging and helping me to see the pieces of the puzzle and, at long last, the puzzle itself.

Donna Ashworth: your poetry inspires me and I appreciate you allowing us to use part of your poem "Joy Chose You," from *Wild Hope*, in the epigraph.

I'm truly indebted to the many individuals I interviewed over the past two years: Howard Axelrod, Moshe Bar, Leslie Barker, Taylor Brorby, Danielle Casioppo, Chip Conley, Scott Davis, David de Souza, Bridget Devlin, John Gaydos, Cathy Hankla, Alex Harris, Vanessa Inn, Matthew Kuan Johnson, Michael Kocet, Jason Konner, Julie Liss, Charles Mathewes, Wallace J. Nichols, Steven Overly, Sarah Porwoll, Adam Smiley Poswolsky, Adam Potkay, Margaret Sartor, Walter Schubert, and Matt Stevens.

In particular, I want to call out "do nothing" Jeff Warren, an expert on so much who taught me a great deal about finding joy in this world and in our hearts, even when the days are dark and short.

Many dear friends stood with me—in Hillsborough and Blowing Rock, N.C., Washington, D.C., San Francisco, New York, and elsewhere—during the two years in which this book came to life. Words can never express how appreciative I am of you all.

A special subset of friends and colleagues helped me in some very specific ways with the book itself: Ann Alexander, Amy Barr, Jo Ann Hallmark, Peter Stein, Simone Weissman, and Elizabeth Woodman. Matt Arion (better known as my Apple Buddy) has helped with tech issues—big and small—for fifteen years. Finally, a huge hug to Julie's lifelong friends—Jenny Schiff Berg, Michele Plaut, and Diane Werder—who filled in my memory gaps with love and stories. (And herewith a sincere apology to anyone I've mistakenly omitted.)

My niece Jessie Petrow-Cohen read and commented brilliantly on the final draft, proving to me, again, the importance of nepotism.

Some of the writing of *The Joy You Make* took place at the Virginia Center for the Creative Arts, and as always, I'm grateful for the gifts of time and space that VCCA provides to hundreds of writers, visual artists, and composers each year. A special shout-out to Sheila Gulley Pleasants, who served as director of artists services at VCCA for an amazing thirty-five years before retiring this past June.

My sister and several members of our family benefited from the many excellent services that the Clearity Foundation provides to those with ovarian cancer and their loved ones. (I'm talking about you, Whitney Read.) Thanks, as well, to my longtime therapist, Phil Spiro. Yes, it takes a village.

Suzanne Somers doesn't belong on a list, which is why she gets her own paragraph. She exuded joy, and I miss her.

Family is everything. Long before Julie became sick, we'd learned to support each other, laugh at each other (I mean with each other), and do so much more. During her long illness, we leaned heavily upon each other, sharing our pain and yes, our joys. I love you all—Julie's wife of thirty-five years, Maddy, and their two daughters, Jessie and Caroline. Ditto to my brother, Jay, his wife, Nancy, and their two "kids," Anna and William. I am beyond fortunate to have such a supportive family.

And then, of course, there's Julie. I like to imagine that she—feisty and fearless, with a smile forever bright—is seeking new adventures and new delights, her laugh echoing across time and space and in the hearts of those who had the privilege to know her. Safe travels, little sister. I love you.